IMPS OF T
PERVER

IMPS OF THE PERVERSE
Gay Monsters in Film

MICHAEL WILLIAM SAUNDERS

PRAEGER

Westport, Connecticut
London

Library of Congress Cataloging-in-Publication Data

Saunders, Michael William, 1953–
    Imps of the perverse : gay monsters in film / Michael William
Saunders.
      p.   cm.
    Includes bibliographical references and index.
    ISBN 0–275–95761–6 (alk. paper)
    1. Homosexuality in motion pictures. I. Title.
PN1995.9.H55S28   1998
791.43′653—dc21   97–33242

Library of Congress Catalog Card Number: 97–33242
ISBN: 0–275–95761–6

First published in 1998

Praeger Publishers, 88 Post Road West, Westport, CT 06881
An imprint of Greenwood Publishing Group, Inc.

Printed in the United States of America

The paper used in this book complies with the
Permanent Paper Standard issued by the National
Information Standards Organization (Z39.48–1984).

10 9 8 7 6 5 4 3 2 1

Copyright Acknowledgments

The author and publisher gratefully acknowledge permission for use of the following material:

Excerpts from *The Cinematic Body* by Steven Shapiro, vol. 2 (Minneapolis: University of Minnesota Press, 1993), pages 167, 175, and 179. Copyright © 1993 by the Regents of the University of Minnesota. Reprinted by permission of University of Minnesota Press.

Transcript of the author's telephone interview with Todd Haynes, January 16, 1995, is printed with the permission of Todd Haynes.

Contents

Acknowledgments

As small and perhaps as inconsiderable a volume as this one is, it could not have come into being without the support and input of a great many people. First I must thank my mentors and advisors at the University of Georgia. Dr. Joel Black's assurances that I had something to say that was worth hearing supported me when my own courage failed. Dr. Charles Eidsvik's sharp and wicked imagination got me started on my little tirade. Dr. Ron Bogue and Dr. Betty Jean Craige listened to me patiently and made me hone some of my better ideas into the occasional coherent sentence. And Dr. Hugh Ruppersburg questioned me about my ideas in a way that helped me state at least some of them more clearly.

At the Georgia Institute of Technology, Dr. Kenneth Knoespel, Dr. Sandra Corse, Dr. Carol Senf, Dr. Jay Telotte and Dr. Blake Leland read or listened to readings from my manuscript and helped me probe further into the darkness I was trying to map.

Constant encouragement during the writing of my manuscript came from my closest friends and my family. Dr. Don Latham, fellow film nut, incomparable wit and tireless advisor, read my manuscript and talked with me almost every day for a year while I worked on the first version of my manuscript. My mother, Annette Gunter Saunders Crotta, also provided steady support and what proved to be my mantra during the ordeal of writing: "This too shall pass, son." My Aunt Hilda Mae Gunter Dyches and my Uncle Clinton Dyches gave me constant encouragement; most especially, my Uncle Clinton told me stories about the movies that made me want to know more. My best friends of many years—Doug Quarterman, Robert McCabe, Delia and Bill Foy, and Howard Shapiro—also listened, argued and helped me smooth out at least some of the rough spots in my thinking. My partner, Cary Jackson, proofread the manuscript and put up with me while I was working through the last stages of the book's production.

With the help of Brad Lapin I got access to films I never would have been able to see otherwise, and I also got a tireless debate partner for the job of continuing to hash out my ideas. With the help of Cliff Bostock I kept scribbling until my manuscript took a more authentic shape.

My thanks also must go to directors Todd Haynes and Rosa Von Praunheim, who allowed themselves to be interviewed for this project and who commented generously about my ideas.

Finally, I could not have come this far had I not had encouragement and guidance from my editors, Nina Pearlstein and Gillian von Beebe. Nina believed I had a good idea for a book and guided me towards getting the whole thing ready to publish; and Gillian helped patiently as I struggled to finish. For all the help I have received from the people who have urged me along, I am sincerely grateful.

CHAPTER 1

A Genealogy
of Gay Monstrosity

As I read and hear about political issues that affect lesbians and gay men currently, it strikes me how much the political climate of the late-nineties resembles that of the early seventies. As in the early seventies, when gay people were becoming visible in unprecedented ways, in the late nineties gay people are, by virtue of their insistence on becoming more visible in the culture at large, the focus of controversy that often affirms that gay people are a threat to the social order. The main issues connected with the visibility of gay people these days are the sanctioning of gay people serving openly in the military and the recognition of same-sex marriages. In the wake of the actions that have been taking place in Hawaii to award full legal recognition to such marriages, conservative politicians, who now control the United States government (as in the early seventies under the Nixon Administration), have latched onto the issue of recognizing same-sex marriages as constituting a threat to family values, while the courts are being left to figure out what the United States government meant when it developed the "don't ask, don't tell" policy concerning gays who serve in the armed forces.

In contrast to the debate of the seventies, one doesn't hear too many conservatives suggesting anymore that gay people should be thrown in jail or committed to mental hospitals. Their argument seems instead to say basically this: We can accept that being gay might be a private matter that is nobody's business as long as it remains a private matter, and as long as it does, we won't worry about whether any harm is being done. However, if "we" conservatives allow being gay to become a public matter by saying through public institutions (like the law) that being gay is not a problem and that it is legitimate to sanction intimate relationships between gay people or the inclination to form such relationships, then society at large is in danger. More specifically, if we say that we will publicly sanction gay relationships and the full participation of gay people in society, then we endanger the integrity of *traditional* families, we endanger national security, and we put the society at large in the position of giving its assent to a way of living that is fundamentally immoral.

The interesting thing to me about this argument is how it rests so simply on the notion that the visibility of gay people is what makes them dangerous. As long as *we* don't admit we see them, gay people aren't all that much of a threat. As long as *they* keep their sexuality private, we can admit that they can do good jobs for their employers and contribute responsibly to the welfare of the nation. It is when gay people insist on being seen, on being recognized and then left to go about their business unmolested, that they represent a threat to social order. As long as *they* don't insist that we see them, *we* can pretend that they don't figure in the shaping of society.

What this argument seems to affirm is that the visibility of gay people is a *monstrous* thing in the most traditional senses of the word. Aside from a few of the more extreme conservatives—like Jesse Helms, Pat Robertson and Strom Thurmond—you don't hear anyone coming close to saying explicitly that homosexuality itself is monstrous; perhaps some would even be shocked at hearing such a pronouncement associated with them, but there it is: What makes homosexuality dangerous is looking at it, admitting we can see it.

The idea of the monster derives from two fundamental etymological myths: that monsters are anomalous creatures that serve as signs indicating the consequences of deviating from the natural order (Look what happens when you do bad things!); and that monsters are marvelous, monumental manifestations of the power of God (Look what God can do!). The monster is, by its very nature, most fundamentally an image whose purpose is to reveal the power and, more importantly, the *terror*, of divinity. As such, it is meant to be seen, but its nature as image is to discourage us, either through fear or through awe, from looking too long where we ought not to look. To retain its power as such an image, then, the monster must be treated as an element of carefully designed rituals. If we look at such an image too long or too often, we commit a sacrilege or we endanger ourselves by presuming to look casually at what we are not meant to be able to bear. As an image, a monster functions to give power to an elect—the hierophants who are allowed to wield the image because they have proven their immunity against it—over those of us who are likely, out of sheer weakness and at any moment, to run off and worship the devil if we aren't watched over carefully.

I don't think it will surprise many gay people to consider the idea that they are viewed widely as monsters, even in these enlightened times, a time of Gay Disney nights and Log Cabin Republicans. Gay people these days know well how dangerous is the idea of their being visible. Oddly, however, people don't seem to talk very explicitly (again, outside of the circles of the far right) about the notion that being gay is still, in these enlightened times, fundamentally viewed as being monstrous. That gay people themselves don't talk much about this fact is, perhaps, an indication of how clear it is to them that their being monstrous is an obvious assumption, deeply embedded within the national psyche, around which they've learned to move. Even among gay people themselves one hears objections to the excessive visibility of gay people: same-sex couples holding hands in the grocery store or smooching as they come out of a movie theater constitute, according to some of my own gay acquaintances, a provocation that is certain to lead the scions of heterosexuality, one of these days, to end up herding us all into a ghetto. Even among gay people, many of whom have fled to the ample lawns and lower tax base of the suburbs, being *seen* as gay is more than unnecessary: it is provocative, if not downright trashy.

A number of thoughts arise as I consider the power of being gay and being visible. One thing that fascinates me in this connection is how other images once considered powerfully monstrous have lost their power or have been transformed into more friendly images. Religious images that bear the function of depicting monstrosity—the image of the Devil, portents of the coming of the Rapture—have ceased, outside of certain sections of Texas and Montana, to have the power that they had for centuries. The image of Satan, outside of fundamentalist congregations, is something of a joke because the power of evil it defines is something we are not inclined anymore to believe in (think of Manservant Hecubus of the "Kids in the Hall" television series). Our own secular history has shown us clearly that there are far more immediate dangers than Beelzebub, while portents and prodigies, which, in the past, also had the effect of performing as monstrous images, no longer have much currency either.

Even secular images of monstrosity have been rendered more or less harmless: it is hard to think of a seriously scary movie version of *Frankenstein* being produced in the current cultural climate; what we get instead is something like the hilarious bit of foolishness offered recently by Kenneth Branagh in *Mary Shelley's Frankenstein*, stinking with music video excess, criminal overacting and leaving us, after all, with the sense that the people telling us the story this time are just having to work too hard at making it all have an impact. All the other (by now) old images of monstrosity—zombies, changelings, space aliens, killer insects—appear more often than not as ironic versions of themselves, as parodic images or as funnymen (as in Tim Burton's 1996 film, *Mars Attacks!*). In fact, in a good many films these days the image of the monster has been domesticated, reduced either to comic figure or to an exposed fake. And this is true, I believe, most simply because our culture has so fully exposed us to such images that we have come finally to either befriend or to be bored by the images that were created to scare us and to warn us to move away. These days, real terror is a nightly feature on the TV news, and it would seem that, as Don

DeLillo predicted in his dark parody *Mao II*, even terrorism is becoming old hat.[1]

In other words, it is very rare to find in fictional literature or film a monstrous image, either one being newly created or one presented from an old narrative, that we are inclined to experience with the force of terror or awe that would have been possible as recently as a generation ago. To the extent that monsters still have the power to really frighten us, they tend these days to appear in the form of real human beings—like Hannibal Lechter—who have forsaken the social contract in the pursuit of madness as a way of life, as a profession, or as a leisure activity. The space aliens and goons who would have had the power to scare the bejezus out of us about a generation ago just don't seem to have the power their older cousins had. The last time I remember being really, horribly scared by a longleggitie beasty (at least in a movie theater) was when I saw *Alien* in 1979: after seeing the movie alone, I checked underneath my car before I got in it to go back home. Hannibal Lechter wasn't all that bad—he could have stewed Jodie Foster's goose, but he just liked her too much.

The experience of such power in the face of a monstrous image is something that is difficult to imagine these days; we've seen all the monsters our culture can dream up, it seems, over and over again, and perhaps we've finally come to think they're not so tough after all. These days the high-tech creatures of movies like *Species* have an oddly unaffecting character. So carefully designed to look truly strange and menacing, they give the impression of being works of such *pure* design that I don't think it is very easy to get beyond looking at them as purely formal exercises in image-making. The last hurrah for high-tech movie monsters may have been the mean and hungry dinosaurs in Steven Spielberg's *Jurassic Park*; it cost so much to bring those critters to life, however, that it doesn't seem likely that we'll be seeing many more of their kind, especially given how many times recently Hollywood studios have lost money on big-budget productions built around special effects (à la *Waterworld*). Even the best of the highest-tech monsters seem oddly devoid of something like internal substance, something like spirit, and this will inevitably mean that such images will tend to have an ever shorter shelf life, moving quickly from the big screen to the video store to the bargain bin. *ET* had a successful second commercial release; I don't think that *Jurassic Park* will.[2]

Of course, what has made this time possible—a time of friendly, even charming talking dragons (as seen most recently in the disappointingly—excuse me—half-hearted *Dragonheart*), fashionably sexy, love-besotted Draculas (as in Gary Oldman's entertaining but somehow disappointing effort in Francis Ford Coppola's *Bram Stoker's Dracula*), goofy or just plain flat Frankensteins and avuncular (*Terminator Two*) cyborgs—is the movie industry itself. The monster movie has been with us since almost the beginning of the motion picture industry; one could easily argue that we have been able, in less than a hundred years, to confront all manner of demon, prodigy, and portent and live to tell the tale to a degree that no other time in human culture has allowed. One might even argue that the monster movie business has served like no other section of the movie industry—with the possible exception of action movies—to bring through technology more devices to create the illusion of realism in movies than has any other genre. Certainly no genre other than the monster movie has been driven more furiously by the absolute necessity of making things look real. As we have become increasingly familiar with our monsters, we have demanded with ever greater hunger to see them look *more* real, to see blood that looks gorier, fangs that slice more menacingly, and the industry has answered with more believable gizmos to convince us that the horror we're seeing is real. Just as the monster movie industry has brought us more of this peculiar sort of realism, however, it has propelled us further into a state of mind in which we could more fully assimilate the notion that a monster looks pretty convincing and not be done in by it. More realism has, in effect, served more fully to tame the monsters in our minds. Paradoxically, the better the monster movie business has gotten, the more it has served to de-claw the monsters our culture creates; perhaps it has served to help us deflate the whole notion of monstrosity.

For all of these reasons, it is all the more significant to find a space in our culture where images still have something of the force of monstrosity. Again, the movies are the place to look, for it is here that we find the greatest abundance of images being created as expressions of the popular imagination. The movies and quite particularly monster movies (as David Skal has interestingly argued recently in his book, *The Monster Show*) are an expression of what's on our minds—especially the dark things. Here again, to return to the point I was making earlier, the image of gay people provides us with an instructive example of what our culture seems to be thinking and feeling at the moment. Two things are remarkable to me in this connection: first, how generally invisible gay people are in the movies, and second, at least in the images created by a certain number of filmmakers, how the kinds of images that are appearing seem to play with the idea of depicting gay people as monsters. What I find in these images is an interesting, very powerful, and yet dangerously tentative expression of the monstrousness of being gay—presented not from the point of view of mainstream culture but rather from that of gay people themselves.

In the pages to follow, I propose to look first at how Hollywood has constructed images of monstrosity, then to look at how gay people have been presented by traditional, Hollywood movies as being, in some sense, monstrous, and finally to turn to a small group of films that seem to appropriate the traditional sense of monstrosity and turn it against itself. What I find in these last films are numerous images that focus very effectively on the idea that being gay is monstrous and that invite gay people to see through this monstrousness—to see that what lies within the image of the monster is often an image of power and humanity that asks us to engage in the world as creative beings.

To understand how the notion of monstrosity works in relation to images of gay people, it is important to begin by talking about what happened with images of gay people as a result of the Gay Liberation movement of the late sixties and early seventies. Gay activists during this period began to scrutinize the media out of concern within the more clearly political arms of the movement (such as the National Gay Task Force) for the way that gays were portrayed (or ignored) in movies, television and print media. For example, when director William Friedkin's film *The Boys in the Band* was released in 1969, it was greeted with condemnation by openly gay critics, who found the movie's stereotypical portrayals of vicious, self-loathing homosexuals not just negative, but also deeply destructive. By 1979, the release of Friedkin's *Cruising* met with highly publicized boycotts by gay political groups, who feared that the movie's depiction of gays as sadistic murderers could spur violence (which fears, in fact, were realized in the murders of two gay men shortly after the film opened[3]). Interestingly, recent criticism of *Cruising* has sought to reclaim the film as being gay-positive.[4]

During the seventies and on into the early eighties, groups like the National Gay Task Force and individuals such as Parker Tyler (in his landmark book on film treatments of homosexuality, *Screening the Sexes: Homosexuality in the Movies*, first published in 1972) and Vito Russo (in his book, *The Celluloid Closet: Homosexuality in the Movies*, first published in 1981) began to map and criticize extensively the political implications of media treatments (primarily in fictional film and television) of homosexuality. Tyler's book, appearing early in the development of gay liberation, focuses on two general observations: that the media tended to portray homosexuals in negative terms (the homosexual as criminal misfit, as comic figure, or as tragic character) and that there emerged a number of cinematic forms that homosexuals were able to appropriate as positive or creative images (primarily through camp images and through subversive readings of fictional film modes). Russo's book, appearing roughly a decade later than Tyler's, focused first on the long history of negative stereotyping of homosexuals in mainstream film and television and concluded (in the revised, 1987 edition) by documenting a new trend in mainstream and underground film and television that portrayed homosexuals in more positive terms. What enabled Russo to document this trend was the appearance in the seventies and eighties of a new body of film work by straight and, more significantly, by openly gay artists dealing with homosexual characters.

What Russo had found in the history of Hollywood was a vast body of images that both indicated and *maintained* traditional beliefs in mainstream culture (both inside and outside America, with America leading the pack in the production of negative images) about the *monstrous* nature of homosexuality. Painstakingly citing the many instances of homosexuals depicted as monsters in film, Russo notes:

Gays were often created [in film] as monsters. In her review of John Flynn's *The Sergeant* (1968), Pauline Kael points out that Rod Steiger's gay soldier isn't *just* homosexual—he's psychopathic—and part of that has to do with his appearing in "normal" surroundings. "Why," she asked, "are all the other soldiers so incredibly, so antiseptically straight that it really begins to look as if you *did* have to be crazy to be homosexual? In this army situation, there is nothing in the atmosphere that links up with the Sergeant's homosexuality ... and homosexuality is, to all appearances, unknown and without cause [so that] it does begin to seem as if only a monster could have such aberrant impulses."[5]

It is worth mentioning here that the context within which *The Sergeant* appeared was the Hollywood of the sixties, the first decade that saw the widespread decline of the production code that had, since the early thirties, carefully censored virtually any mention of homosexuality in films that appeared in the United States. According to Russo, it was director Otto Preminger who, in 1961, maneuvered the Motion Picture Association of America (MPAA) into relaxing its refusal to allow depictions of homosexuality to appear on the screen, thereby permitting Preminger, with his film *Advise and Consent* (1961), to present to American audiences one of the most explicit treatments of homosexuality in almost thirty years. Russo argues that it was only possible, at this point in Hollywood history, to get the censors to allow the screening of those depictions of homosexuality that showed gay men and lesbians as being abnormal, diseased, doomed to self destruction or hopelessly criminal in character. Thus, somewhat ironically, these first depictions of homosexuals in the sixties—such as in *Advise and Consent*, where the homosexual-identified character commits suicide out of self-loathing and later, in *The Sergeant*, where, as Kael puts it, the homosexual character is depicted openly as a monstrous aberration—actually represent an intermediate stage of progress towards a more measured discussion in film of homosexuality, because at least they begin to undo what Hollywood had done for so long—conceal the subject of homosexuality under innuendo and carefully coded circumlocution.

The images that emerged in the "relaxed" sixties, however, only openly stated what Hollywood had already been saying in coded language for the past thirty years or so. In this connection, Russo observes: "In the sixties lesbians and gay men were pathological, predatory and dangerous; villains and fools, but never heroes."[6] As evidence of this trend, here is a selection from the list of sixties films Russo cites: *A Walk on the Wild Side* (directed by Edward Dmytryk, 1962), featuring Barbara Stanwyck as a predatory lesbian madam; *The Servant* (Joseph Losey, 1963), featuring James Fox and Dirk Bogarde in a sadomasochistic, master-slave relationship; *The Fearless Vampire Killers* (Roman Polanski, 1968) featuring a ludicrous gay vampire; *The Detective* (Gordon Douglas, 1968), centered around a series of grisly gay mutilation murders; *The Fox* (Mark Rydell, 1968), depicting Anne Heywood being "saved" from a lesbian relationship with Sandy Dennis by the ministrations of Keir Dullea and by the fatal, "fortunate fall" of a tree onto Dennis; and *Staircase* (Stanley Donen, 1969), in which Rex Harrison and Richard Burton play aged, comically bickering homosexual lovers. What these images reveal explicitly is, for Russo, a closely related series of character types that had already, as early as the thirties (after the imposition of the production code) frequently been used by filmmakers to code characters as implying their homosexuality through various aspects of monstrosity.

These aspects of character appeared generally in earlier films through three fictional modes: comedy of manners, detective fiction (especially film noir) and horror films. The weakest form of monstrous character appeared in comedies (especially thirties screwball comedies) as the sissy, a form in which character actors like Franklin Pangborn and Edward Everett Horton excelled. For Russo, the sissy appears usually as the central male character's butler or as a minor character with whom the central male character comes into comic conflict. In this context, the sissy indicates homosexuality obliquely by depicting "symbols for failed masculinity [which] therefore did not represent the threat of actual homosexuals"[7]; that is, the sissy simply functions to provide a comic deformation of the male lead's successful pursuit of the film's principal female character. Said yet another way, the sissy butler or hotel manager was not trying to seduce the male lead; he was, rather, simply a bungling, comic counterpart to the male lead's search for proper love, which is to say, love with a real girl.

What Russo seems to overlook in such depictions has to do with the nature of the sissy as not merely comic but also ugly image. Character actors such as Edward Everett Horton and Franklin Pangborn *look* funny, both in that they look comic and in that they look, in a real sense, *deformed*. Much of both actors' appeal (and they represent a type that flourished well beyond the thirties) consisted of their talents for using comic gesture (hands on hips, hands fluttering about the face confusedly, and so forth) and exaggerated facial expression to indicate their haplessness, particularly in the "face" of the male lead's superior ability in navigating through a romance. Horton and Pangborn worked quite obviously to capitalize on their ability to deform themselves, particularly by exaggerating facial expressions, to indicate not merely what Russo calls "failed masculinity," but furthermore to indicate that that failure itself is a visible, which is to say (certainly within the context of film) a *real* deformity. The essence of the comic is, as Aristotle formulates it, most fundamentally a form of the ridiculous that expresses itself as ugliness.[8] Critical tradition may assert that comic ugliness is, as Aristotle says, "not painful or destructive"; however, this type of ugliness is still experienced as a deformity, albeit of a milder sort. Searching among other film genres, we find that the comic ugliness of the sissy takes more intense forms.

In contrast to comedy, detective films of the thirties, forties and fifties, especially film noir, employ ugliness as a code for homosexuality in a way that both incorporates and intensifies comic ugliness. In films such as *The Maltese Falcon* (directed by John Huston, 1941) for example, Peter Lorre (who had attained stardom and an early pattern of type-casting playing a child murderer in Fritz Lang's *M*, released in 1931), portrays a fastidious sissy who is also (along with character actor Elisha Cook, Jr.) the underling of the far more sinister character portrayed by Sidney Greenstreet. Concerning the gangster's underling, a stock character in hard-boiled detective fiction (from which film noir drew much of its stories), Russo makes the following observations: "Since about 1915, bums and prisoners had used the German word *gansel* or *gosling*, corrupted to *gunsel*, for a passive sodomite, especially a young, inexperienced boy companion. From the twenties it gradually came to mean a sneaky or disreputable person of any kind. By the thirties it meant petty gangster or hoodlum."[9] Thus a character like Lorre's in *The Maltese Falcon* presents the fastidious sissy who provides more than mere comic diversion. As he stumbles through his conflict with Humphrey Bogart's Sam Spade, Lorre's character, exotically named Joel Cairo, appears at first to be no major threat to Sam Spade. In one scene, where Lorre surprises Bogart in his office, he is summarily overpowered with a single slap in the face, despite his having a gun, which he later admits is not even loaded. Lorre's character does pose a threat to Bogart, however, in the way he functions as an intermediary between Bogart and Greenstreet, Lorre's boss and the most dangerous character in the film. Coded in the film as a homosexual who leads Bogart into the criminal underworld, Lorre points the way to danger, possibly to death. Again in this film Lorre's character is made to appear comically ugly in his fastidiousness and in his puny ineffectuality before Bogart's unquestionable manhood, but the comic value of this ugliness on Lorre's part is undercut, turned into something more ugly and therefore less comic, by virtue of his connection with a very real threat of violence.

The connection in mainstream film between implied homosexuality and criminality tends, in films of the forties and fifties, to take much stronger forms than that seen in Huston's film. For example, in Alfred Hitchcock's *Rope* (1948) and *Strangers on a Train* (1951) the director pairs two elegant young men in a murder pact (in *Rope*, which was inspired by the infamous Loeb-Leopold murder case) based on the conspirators' deranged belief in their own intellectual superiority or (in *Strangers on a Train*) by the conspirators' sociopathic desire to extricate themselves from domestic entanglements. Concerning the latter film, in which Farley Granger and Robert Walker play the two young men, Russo observes:

> [Robert] Walker's choice [to play his character as a homosexual] was particularly exciting in terms of the plot. The tension it created between his malignantly fey Bruno and Granger's golly gee tennis player, Guy Haines, heightened the bizarre nature of their pact. Bruno would kill Guy's unwanted wife, and in exchange Guy would murder Bruno's hated father. Bruno's homosexuality emerged in terms that would be used increasingly throughout the Fifties to define gays as aliens. His coldness, his perverse imagination and an edge of elitist superiority made him an extension of the sophisticated but deadly sissy played by Clifton Webb in *Laura*, Peter Lorre in *The Maltese Falcon* and Martin Landau in *North by Northwest*.[10]

By referring to Walker's portrayal of the character Bruno as "malignantly fey," Russo comes just short of indicating something important about the specifically *visual* character of that portrayal. At several points in the film, Hitchcock shoots Walker in a distorted, low or oddly angled close-up in such a way as to empha- size several characteristics of Walker's face. These shots emphasize at one and the same time Walker's youthful appearance and a look of deranged detachment that serves as a subtle, horrific counterpoint to the actions his character is en- gaged in: getting rid of dad, dragging another young man into an unspeakable crime. Similarly, Farley Granger is shot frequently in close-up to emphasize his elegant boyishness: as he struggles with the temptation to *yield* to Bruno, Guy plays out his crisis before us primarily in terms of facial expressions, expres- sions that play on themes of melancholy and distress (but rarely remorse). By focusing in these ways on specific aspects of the young man's face, Hitchcock is able to effect yet another level of meaning to the elegant sissy's character, one that couples a heightened sense of youthful male beauty with a sense of perni- cious inner sickness.[11]

Through these films—the comedies of the thirties, film noir and suspense films of the forties and fifties—we can see a progression of the sissy from a comic deformation of maleness to a deeply sinister, overt *perversion* of male- ness. As the sissy becomes more closely identified with violence, he expresses a fear in the popular imagination that homosexuality *is* violence. The violence that is indicated here is more than the violence of specific acts, sexual or other- wise: it is the violence that homosexuality is believed to do against the natural order itself—the way homosexuality is made to function as a sign for peril in the normal order of things. Because it is nature that the homosexual attacks by virtue of his mere existence, he must be constructed as being not merely bad but rather, as Russo puts it, as being "alien." This alien character codes the homo- sexual as being a threat to the natural order of things, which is to say, as being a monster.

If comedies, film noir and suspense films code homosexuals as monsters, they are, for the most part, social monsters: effeminate men, petty gangsters, and dangerous sociopaths. The films of the thirties, forties and fifties tended to use specific visual elements to express the monstrosity of these characters: the comic ugliness of the befuddled sissy's face, the suspiciously androgynous look of the gunsel, and the vacuous, affectless look of the too-beautiful, elegant kil- ler. In yet another genre of this period, the horror film, the homosexual is coded as a monster in a necessarily much more explicitly visual way.

As one surveys the corpus of the horror film genre, one is struck by the way that homosexual characters appear. First, overtly male homosexual monsters rarely appear in horror films as major characters. Films that do depict such characters are, for the most part, borderline horror films: containing significant elements of horror, these films generally defy being classified neatly as horror films in the tradition of *Dracula* or *Frankenstein*. Arguably the first such char- acter in mainstream film is that of Sebastian Venable in *Suddenly Last Summer* (directed by Joseph Mankiewicz, 1959). This example is already problematic, because Manckiewizc's film, which focuses on psychological horror stemming from events the audience can recognize as being "real" rather than supernatural, brackets its presentation of horror as an admittedly artificial construction. That is, whereas in "pure" horror films the monster is literally present as an alien creature whose actual existence is consistent with the film's cosmology, in Mankiewicz's film the monster, the predatory homosexual poet Sebastian, is "present" only as a symbolic value, an indicator for the "real" mind's suscepti-bility to derangement. Thus Sebastian is never seen fully in the film; the only surviving image that depicts the character who played him is a publicity shot, showing a sinisterly androgynous young man looking at one and the same time fey and menacing as he stands against a white stucco wall, his large, rather clawlike hands prominently folded across his chest. The nature of Sebastian's presence in the film leads me to believe that he is meant to be seen as an in-stance of the sublime: the idea of the predatory homosexual, the film suggests, is too much for us to be able to take in, and so it must be hinted at, brought to us in small chunks (an occasional view of Sebastian's leg or of his shadow cast along a wall).

In director Roman Polanski's *The Fearless Vampire Killers* (1967), we find a gay vampire who is clearly constructed as a comic character (his name is Her-bert, which certainly lacks the horrific ring of Browning's *Dracula* or Murnau's *Nosferatu*), and whose effeminacy clearly undercuts the seriousness of the threat he poses to others. A more overtly menacing male monster is the satanic trans-sexual in Russ Meyer's cult/horror/sexploitation film, *Beyond the Valley of the Dolls* (1979); like Sebastian in *Suddenly Last Summer*, Meyer's killer transie is bracketed as psychological anomaly (he has a psychotic breakdown and goes on a killing spree) that approaches the supernatural in its physical aspects (during his spree, he reveals he has a woman's breasts). A recent instance of a male ho-mosexual as monster in a horror film is that of the character of the serial killer in director Jonathan Demme's *The Silence of the Lambs* (1991) in which a genuinely menacing homosexual serial killer constructs a monstrous outer shell for himself from the skins of the women he murders. Significantly, this charac-ter was viewed by many gay audiences as being such a completely stereotypical vision of the homosexual as monster as to warrant numerous public actions de-crying the film's characterization of the killer. Also significant is the fact that the film was quite popular.

If overt depictions of male homosexual monsters are rare in horror films, it is interesting to compare such depictions with those of female horror-film mon-sters. When lesbians appear as monsters, they typically appear as vampires (e.g., *Dracula's Daughter* directed by Lambert Hillyer, 1936, possibly the first more or less explicit depiction of the overtly gay monster in a horror film; *Blood and Roses,* Roger Vadim, 1961; the infamous series of sexploitation lesbian vampire films produced by the British Hammer Studios, including *The Vampire Lovers,* Roy Baker, 1970, *Twins of Evil,* John Hough, 1971, and *Lust for a Vampire,* Jimmy Sangster, 1971; *The Hunger*, Tony Scott, 1983, and *Nadja*, Michael Almereyda, 1994) or as supernatural or virtually superhuman predators who resemble vampires in their lust for blood (e.g., *Cat People,* Jacques Tourneur, 1942, and arguably, *Basic Instinct,* Paul Verhoeven, 1992).

What stands out immediately as we compare lesbian monsters with gay male monsters in the lists given here is first, that the former are more common than the latter, and second, that for the most part lesbian monsters are constructed as being more powerfully threatening than are gay male monsters. While Russo argues that the monsters of James Whale's *Frankenstein* and *Bride of Frankenstein* can be read as metaphors for the status of gay men as aliens in "normal" society,[12] neither he nor any other film historian I have consulted has assembled a list of male homosexual monsters in horror films that goes significantly beyond that listed above. While lesbians appear more often than gay men as horror-film monsters, it is clear that, given the vast number of films that contain significant elements of horror, male homosexual characters are relatively uncommon in such films.

It is not difficult to account for the scarcity of male homosexual monsters in horror film. As Russo documents exceedingly well, the MPAA board of censors worked studiously to excise any mention of homosexuality in films shown in the United States from the early thirties through the late fifties. It was not until directors like Otto Preminger challenged the code as a publicity ploy that the MPAA began to relax its near-total ban on any depiction of homosexual characters in film.[13] Hence, in early horror films like *Dracula's Daughter*, the possibility of lesbian desire *could* be discreetly presented (posters for the film announced: "Save the women of London from Dracula's Daughter!"[14]) within the context of supernatural monstrosity. Because, as Laura Mulvey has pointed out, films have so consistently been constructed from the point of the male gaze,[15] and because lesbian desire has typically been both devalued as female desire and co-opted as serving male desire, it should be no wonder that lesbian characters would be allowed to be presented in horror films at least somewhat more frequently than is true for gay male characters. Saying this is not inconsistent with noting that lesbian horror-film monsters typically appear more powerful than do gay male monsters. If we can accept that the primary point of interest in traditional film is the heterosexual male gaze and the pleasure that underlies it, and if we can agree on the commonness with which images of lesbian desire function as a focus of male heterosexual desire, then it becomes possible to read these powerful lesbian vampires as being first and last images rendered "safe" both because they are rendered as images of women as supernatural beings and because they are images aimed ultimately at serving male desire. Lesbian vampires can be seen by straight men as having power because that vision is not overwhelming—as women they have been defined from the beginning as being essentially powerless. But a (really menacing) gay male vampire? The best way to deal with *him* is to diminish his image by making it appear comic.

Paradoxically, then, traditional film can present a powerful lesbian monster, because the very notion of female power has been discounted from the start. In contrast, the idea of presenting gay male monsters is more dangerous for a variety of reasons. Because gay male identity has for so long been closely identified with stereotypical ideas about the effeminate man and because the sissy so easily becomes a comic figure, it was not until audiences could accept the idea that gay men can look and act just "like real men" that such audiences could be made to view a homosexual man as being a powerful, threatening character. For this change in perception we have World War II to thank, for it was during that social upheaval that many heterosexuals came in contact to an unprecedented degree with homosexuals and began to experience these "others" as real, fully complex people. Or so I am told by my gay friends who served in that war.

Although the period after World War II saw greater openness in discussing the fact of gay identity, gay male figures tended to emerge in the films of the fifties and sixties either as victims (as director Basil Dearden's 1961 film *The Victim* clearly announced) or as pent, crazed criminals (as in *The Sergeant*), but very rarely as truly frightening, engaging monsters. The tendency to depict gay male characters in these roles clearly identified them as a social problem, as a vivid expression of cultural anxiety. These gay male characters were not represented explicitly as monsters of the Frankenstein sort, for such monsters tend to appear as images of a troublesome reality that has been rendered approachable, images that we can accept might be true about ourselves. While heterosexual male lust may be publicly shameful, it may at least be imagined (through a figure like Dracula or the Wolf Man) without breaking the rules of being a man. Because in our society male homosexuality is viewed as breaking those rules (or so it appears), it is, often, too terrible to be imagined, too terrible to be assigned an image.

Of all film genres, horror is arguably the genre most specifically focused on investing much of its dramatic power in specific, narrowly constructed images. We go to see a horror film specifically to *see* the monster; the scenes in which (s)he is *not* present serve primarily to allow us to recharge our nervous system so that we can feel the force of the monster's reappearance.[16] In this genre, the monster's presence is the central focus. The plot's function is to maintain the power of that presence.

Compare, for example, the frequency with which the monster appears in the film versions of *Dracula* and the frequency with which the monster appears in Bram Stoker's novel. In Stoker's novel, Dracula is very rarely present except as an unseen influence acting upon other characters, chiefly Renfield, Lucy Westenra and Mina Harker. The suspense that Stoker creates by keeping Dracula largely unseen leads us as readers to focus on the struggles that other characters experience in dealing with a malevolent force they cannot readily see. In the novel, then, it is the formlessness of the monster that creates and maintains terror.

By contrast, film versions of Stoker's story—undoubtedly one of the most often-filmed stories in film—focus consistently on showing us the monster during much of the film. One might argue here that it makes sense that we see more of the monster in film, because film is, after all, a visual medium. Fine.

Yet, if we consider how some filmmakers, such as Alfred Hitchcock, are able to use the unseen to terrify us (think here of the infamous shower scene in *Psycho*), we must acknowledge that film has developed more than one narrative trope to elicit feelings of terror from an audience. The suspense film genre seeks to tease us into feeling the terror of the unseen; the horror film genre, in clear contrast, obliges us (or allows us) more clearly to *see* the object of our terror.

Thus a great deal of the imagery of horror films plays on the nature of presence. The monster in such films may be an animal anomaly (*King Kong, One Million Years B. C.*); it may be a human creature hideously deformed as a permanent condition (*Nosferatu, Phantom of the Opera, Frankenstein,* or *The Mummy*); it may be a creature that is transformed from (in some instances only apparently) a normal human guise to a visible, supernatural form (*Dracula, White Zombie, Dracula's Daughter, The Wolf Man,* Cocteau's *Beauty and the Beast,* Romero's *Night of the Living Dead*); it may be able to become invisible (*The Invisible Man* or *Dracula,* in which the vampire dissolves into fog and is unable to cast a reflection in mirrors); or, finally, the monster may have an extraterrestrial form, that it may or may not be able to disguise (*War of the Worlds, The Thing, I Married a Monster From Outer Space, Invasion of the Body Snatchers,* and countless other drive-in, science-fiction horror movies). The frequency with which the fact and nature of the monster's appearance are foregrounded in horror films underscores how central the matter of appearance is for the genre, just as the (sometimes explicitly) alien nature of the monster's appearance reveals affinities between it and what we have already found in the imagery of effeminate men in film.

Much of what renders images of sissies proximate to images of monsters has to do with the fact that most monsters in film have been identified as being male. Regarding male-identified monsters in folklore, Bruno Bettelheim convincingly argues that monsters in fairy tales express anxiety on the part of a young girl for the loss of her virginity to a male.[17] In fairy tales, Bettelheim notes, a male monster is a changeling: by day he is a normal man, but at night he turns into a hideous beast, and it is often when such a character appears as a monster that he encounters a young, innocent girl who has been warned about him by an older woman. This warning is a code, Bettelheim contends, for an adult mother's fear that her innocent daughter will be destroyed (she will no longer be a girl) if she loses her virginity. Through this fear, sexuality is identified with loss. Invariably, however, when the young girl actually encounters the monster, she transforms him, usually through a kiss. His transformation reveals him to be a charming prince, the ideal mate for the innocent girl. The fairy tale of this type thus allows the notion of sexuality as threat (from the mother's perspective) to change into sexuality as actualized maturation (from the daughter's perspective). Bettelheim's analysis suggests that images of monsters can express a fear of sexuality, especially male sexuality, and may (perhaps more interestingly) appear in a position proximate to their supposed opposite: that is, in the image of the monster, fear of and delight in sex can appear side by side. In the fairy tale, the monster may become Prince Charming: fear of sex may come to be transformed into the acceptance of mature pleasure.

If the fairy-tale monster provides a medium for resolving fears about sexuality, the horror-movie monster reveals something very different. In the horror film, the monster, whether male- or female-identified, frequently functions as an impediment, a rival preventing the successful union of a good, "normal" man with a woman. Rarely is the horror-movie monster the Other of a sympathetic, male love interest. In a case in which the monster is an alternate form for a sympathetic male character (such as in *The Invisible Man*, *The Wolf Man* or *The Fly*), the "normal" persona is brought to a point where he must prove his faithfulness to his true (female) love by allowing himself (along with his monstrous other self) to be destroyed. Following Bettelheim's logic, this scenario would point to an unresolved retreat into fear of male sexuality. When horror films allow a way out of this retreat, it is by so arranging things that another male, not identified explicitly with the monster, saves an endangered female from the monster's power.

Interestingly, it may be that in the latter case, the male who saves the female character is saving her, at least in part, from *herself*. In early vampire films, for example, (such as *Dracula* and *Dracula's Daughter*) a young girl is often seduced by the vampire: she is unable to resist the supernatural force with which the monster hypnotically draws her to him (or her). Significantly, the girl is unaware of being drawn to the vampire, and the conventions of the cinematic form emphasize that the vampire exerts its greatest power at night, the time of sleep and of the heightened activity of the Unconscious. The logic of such a plot complication implicates the young girl in the monster's unnatural medium of being. With the young girl's collusion brought into the picture, the force of the monster reveals itself no longer to be male sexuality in particular but sexuality itself.

Powerless to help herself, the young girl must be saved by a stouthearted, pure young man who truly, selflessly loves her. To prove his devotion, the young man usually swears an oath with someone who shows him how to save the girl and who may give him an amulet to protect him from the monster. The oath and the amulet define the young man in a way that shows his characterological origins in epic literature: like Aeneas, he confronts the forces of the underworld to find truth, a truth he can receive only if he is virtuous.[18] The young male can only prove his virtue by killing the vampire, whereupon the young girl is released from her hypnotic bondage and is united with her savior. The construction of the plot around salvation clearly points to the way such a fictional form allows the problem of sexuality to be resolved: the monster must be killed, just as lawless sexuality itself must be symbolically killed, for the protagonists to be saved. The truth revealed in confronting the monster here is, putatively at least, that the hypnotic attraction of the monster (lawless sexuality) is an illusion.

Particularly in vampire films, the act of killing the monster is imbued with sexual imagery. The decisive way to dispatch the vampire is by piercing its heart, an act of penetration that recalls the act by which the monster feeds off of and transforms its victims. The vampire's death-penetration at the hands of the virtuous young man is hardly a simple act of destruction. In this act, virtue overwhelms vice through a violent act of homosocial union (between monster and monster-killer).

Despite their focus on the monster's destruction, many monster movies since the early thirties show the dead creature returning to life. The numerous versions of the Dracula story recorded on film, for instance, allow for the monster to be revived if the fatal wooden stake is withdrawn from the desiccated remains. Similarly, the revival of the Frankenstein monster, the cursed mummy or, more recently, the supernaturally powerful psychopath (the character of Freddy Krueger in the *Nightmare on Elm Street* sequels) attests to the monster's ability to return even after he is "destroyed." While such plot devices enable studio "pitch" makers and screenwriters to extend their profits, the fact that audiences accept these devices—witness the popularity of horror film sequels—indicates something deeper about the power of the figure of the monster itself. The willingness of audiences to accept the monster's persistent survival seems most directly to arise from the sexual nature of the monster's power. If killing the monster entails "killing" sexuality, reviving the monster suggests that nothing has really been killed, but rather that what we thought to have buried with the monster cannot die.

Furthermore, the way audiences seem to take pleasure in seeing the monster return belies certain aspects of the audience's fascination. While viewers accept the logic of killing the monster, they are most fascinated with *seeing* the monster; hence, the monster must always be allowed to return. Our fascination in seeing the monster destroyed conceals our desire to see, and to continue to confront, the living monster itself. Something is embedded in the horror of the monster's form and behavior that is not at all horrifying, but rather attractive, exciting. Many film versions of the Dracula story, for instance (including Francis Ford Coppola's *Dracula*, released in 1992), construct the vampire as being simultaneously horrifying and charming. In early versions of the Frankenstein story, the monster is depicted as being, at times, sympathetically childlike (as when, in James Whale's *Frankenstein*, the monster weeps while he listens to a blind man playing the violin) or as being capable of a heroic degree of tragic self-awareness (as when, in Whale's *The Bride of Frankenstein*, the monster, seeing himself spurned by his newly manufactured monster bride, sadly tells his creator "You go! You live! We belong dead!" thereby precipitating a scene of destruction). It has been said of Jean Cocteau's *Beauty and the Beast* (released in 1946) that the monster is more engaging, more attractive than the prince into which he is transformed by Beauty's kiss.[19] And in the more recent "Terminator" movies (*The Terminator*, James Cameron, 1984 and, from the same director, *Terminator Two: Judgment Day* released in 1991), the menacing (beefcake) cyborg portrayed by Arnold Schwarzenegger in the first film of the series is revived, in the second film, as a "kinder, gentler" tragic (beefcake) father figure who commits himself to a fiery death as an act of love benefiting his "adopted" son.

The fact that many horror-film monsters are often revived and, on occasion, "rehabilitated" into less threatening figures, suggests several interesting points of convergence with homosexual film characters who are also presented as being, in some way, monstrous. Looking at "straight" and homosexual monsters, we can see how precariously the monster maintains his or her position as a figure of horror. It is often in the very power of such a figure's monstrosity (as in *King Kong* or *Dracula's Daughter*) that (s)he becomes an object of fascination. We are as fascinated as we are scared at the thought of a giant, wild, overwhelmingly powerful creature holding in his massive paw the object of his desire, a tiny, fragile creature who is no match for him any more than he is for her. A film like *King Kong* can be experienced as a tragic love story because of the sublime incommensurability between the monster and the object of his desire.[20] Similarly, in *Dracula's Daughter*, as in other lesbian vampire films, the monster transgresses the logic of natural and moral law in an explosion of the received notions about socially acceptable, "healthy" forms of erotic desire. There can be little doubt that such images allow us to imagine a degree of freedom that we wouldn't generally dare to act out.

All this leads us to a conclusion that may shed more light onto the relative scarcity of male homosexual monsters in horror films: since monsters are made to be seen, we only make monsters out of what we can bear to look at (our horror often masking fascination, desire, and an appetite for experiencing a sense of awe). Considering that homosexuality has been constructed in Western culture as such a consummately transgressive form of behavior and character, it may appear remarkable that we find so few explicitly gay monsters in the horror film, yet when we consider the many instances in horror films in which, as in the fairy tales described by Bettelheim above, the monster becomes transformed or revived into an overtly desirable character, it may become clearer why male homosexual monsters are such rarities in horror film. Because film is focused so much on expressing male desire, what could be more horrific than images that erase the boundary lines by which maleness defines itself? It is this threat that male homosexuality poses to the male gaze.

I think that all I've said so far about monsters in horror film suggests that such figures have a great subversive potential. They play havoc with the binary pairs of repulsion/desire and terror/fascination, showing the proximate nature of such terms. Moreover, they provide us with a means of playing with our ambivalence about the clash between our private appetites and proper, civilized behavior. Because monsters in traditional horror film illustrate in an extreme form the potential for subverting fundamental values, they point the way to an interesting trend in films.

Precisely because of the threat they pose to the traditional male gaze, gay men rarely appear as explicit monsters. For the same reason, because they are such threatening characters, gay men who do appear in horror films tend to appear as either minor characters (an arguable example being Renfield in Tod Browning's 1931 version of *Dracula*), as ambiguous characters (such as Ernest Thesiger's campy/menacing portrayal of Dr. Pretorius in James Whale's 1932 film, *Bride of Frankenstein*), or as ridiculous ones (like Herbert, the effeminate gay vampire in *The Fearless Vampire Killers*). If the viewer derives a good deal of satisfaction from the monster's character by seeing in him or her the proximity of repulsion and desire, then the rarity of gay male monsters in film indicates that gay male characters do not easily lend themselves to showing that proximity. Given this fact, it will appear as doubly subversive if a filmmaker constructs a gay character in film who is as powerful and as menacing as the monsters of traditional film genres such as the horror film.

In fact, from the forties through the present, a handful of filmmakers—many but not all of them underground artists (including Jean Genet, Kenneth Anger, James Broughton and George Kuchars) have been creating compelling, engaging gay monsters—generally working within the framework of social monstrosity—in independent film. More recently, a growing group of post-Gay Liberation filmmakers (some of them openly gay, such as Rainer Werner Fassbinder, Rosa Von Praunheim, John Waters, Monika Treut, Pedro Almodovar, Todd Haynes, Tom Kalin, Gus Van Sant, Jennie Livingston and others) have focused on presenting monstrous gay characters who depart from the stereotypes of the Hollywood genre films and present us with characters that are engaging and powerful.

The work of these filmmakers is important for a great many reasons. First, both groups challenge much of the ideology implicit to the notion of the assimilation of gay life into the mainstream, and as such, they are as potentially disturbing within as without the gay community. Because gay liberation has put pressure on the media, mainstream film has been obliged, since the early seventies, both to answer for its openly homophobic portrayals of gay people and to produce more positive images of gay people. One effect of this pressure has been to make mainstream films about gay people more bankable, particularly those cast in the mode of love story or comedy (witness the commercial success of Merchant/Ivory's *Maurice* in the eighties and, most recently, of Mike Nichols's *The Bird Cage* in 1996). Another effect of this pressure has been to make it easier for gay filmmakers working independently (such as director Bill Sherwood, who had great success with his 1986 gay romantic comedy, *Parting Glances*) to find financing and enthusiastic audiences for their projects. Thus, while gay activists have had to reckon with homophobic films like Friedkin's *Cruising*, they have also had to deal with the works of certain filmmakers that look dangerously like the homophobic films the mainstream industry has tended to produce.

Perhaps just as important as the philosophical divisions this latter group of monster-makers has precipitated in the gay community (which has always been significantly divided within itself) is the way this group of filmmakers has worked to subvert the very nature of monstrosity as it tends to be constructed in film. What I hope to do in the present study is to show that in the work of a significant number of filmmakers, gay characters are presented in a way that challenges both traditional views of monstrosity and more recent, gay-assimilationist views about the nature of homosexual desire and the place of gay people in the society as a whole. I hope to show that, for some filmmakers, looking at homosexual monsters can give us a way of affirming gay identity and of defying the call to assimilate altogether *invisibly* into mainstream society.

NOTES

1. I can't help but mention here a little anecdote from my own social experience. Recently a friend of mine visited another friend in the hospital. While friend #1 was visiting, the hospital was evacuated because of a bomb scare. In retelling the events of the visit, my friend noted that the hospital had served baked mackerel two days in a row. Hearing this, those of us present at the retelling made no comment about the bomb scare, but we all spontaneously expressed disgust at the thought of hospital fish being offered two days in succession.

2. As of the present writing *The Lost World* (1997), Spielberg's much-ballyhooed sequel to *Jurassic Park*, has had a disappointing box office run.

3. "In November 1980, outside the Ramrod Bar, the site of the filming of *Cruising*, a minister's son emerged from a car with an Israeli machine gun and killed two gay men." Vito Russo, *The Celluloid Closet: Homosexuality in the Movies*. Revised Edition (New York: Harper and Row, 1987), 238.

4. See in particular Bob Stephens's 1995 reappraisal of *Cruising* in a review entitled "Lasting Images of *Cruising*." (Online. The Internet Movie Database), Sept. 10, 1996.

5. Russo, 48.

6. Russo, 122.

7. Russo, 33-4.

8. Aristotle, *Poetics*, *The Complete Works of Aristotle*, Vol. 2 of the Revised Oxford Translation, Jonathan Barnes, ed. (Princeton, N.J.: Princeton University Press, 1990), 2319.

9. Russo, 46-47.

10. Russo, 94.

11. Discussing film treatments of the melancholy young homosexual, Richard Dyer writes: "The sad young man is neither androgynously in-between the genders nor playing with the signs of gender. His relationship to masculinity is more difficult, and thus sad. He is a young man, hence not yet really a real

man. He is soft, he has not yet achieved assertive masculine hardness. He is also physically less than a man." This is as much as saying that the elements of characterization for this type involve a certain deformation of a more generally received notion of "successful" masculinity, which deformation can quite easily be read, especially within the context of Hitchcock's films, as indicating monstrosity. See Richard Dyer, *The Matter of Images: Essays on Representation* (New York: Routledge, 1993), 42.

12. Russo, 49-52.

13. Russo, 61-123.

14. Russo, 49.

15. See Laura Mulvey, "Film and Visual Pleasure," in *Film Theory and Criticism: Introductory Readings*, Gerald Mast and Marshall Cohen, eds. (New York: Oxford University Press, 1985), 803-816.

16. In this connection, Marie Hélène Huet makes some interesting remarks on the genealogy of the concept of monstrosity, beginning with the writings of Saint Augustine:

> Several traditions linked the word monster to the idea of showing or warning. One belief, following Augustine's City of God, held that the word monster derived from the Latin monstrare: to show, to display (montrer in French). Monster, then, belongs to the etymological family that spawned the word demonstrate as well. For Renaissance readers, this tradition confirmed the idea that monsters were signs sent by God, messages showing his will or his wrath, though Fortunio Liceti gave it a simpler meaning in 1616: 'Monsters are thus named, not because they are signs of things to come, as Cicero and the Vulgate believed ... but because they are such that their new and incredible appearance stirs admiration and surprise in the beholders, and startles them so much that everyone wants to show them to others [se les monstre réciproquement].' Another tradition, the one adopted by current etymological dictionaries, derived the word monster from monere, to warn.

See Huet, *Monstrous Imagination,* (Cambridge: Harvard University Press, 1993), 6.

17. See Bruno Bettelheim, *The Uses of Enchantment: The Meaning and Importance of Fairy Tales* (New York: Vintage Books, 1977), 297.

18. Northrop Frye, *Anatomy of Criticism* (Princeton: Princeton University Press, 1973), 321.

19. Francis Steegmuller, *Cocteau: A Biography* (Boston: Little, Brown and Company, 1970), 358.

20. Joseph Campbell contends that monsters are images of the sublime and that our awe before the sublime explains much of our fascination with them. See Campbell, *The Power of Myth,* (New York: Doubleday, 1988), 157.

CHAPTER 2

Growing Up Monstrous:
My Own Private Idaho
and *The Living End*

Somewhere I remember hearing a gay man say that he learned to be a man by learning how not to be a girl. What struck me about this statement is the way it seems to shed light on a feature of maleness that people seem either to overlook or to consider unfit for polite company: that defining maleness is very much a process of negation, that denial is the engine that drives the establishing of maleness. It's a commonplace that men deny being emotional, feeling pain and fear—embedded into that commonplace is a profoundly important feature of defining identity that people rarely seem to admit—perhaps because, as part of the firmament in which our notion of maleness is suspended, this feature is something we are not supposed to examine. What irony there is here: the notion of establishing—a process of affirmation—is contained within a system of valuation that proceeds by denying—a process of subtraction. To proceed into maleness, we must subtract, take away—when we're through taking things away, we have a genuine male, a real man.

The process of subtraction we call initiation. We commonly hear it said, in connection with the rites of initiation, that to be made into a man, a boy must first be broken down or toughened up—as in boot camp. What can be affirmed in him as man must arise from what is taken away from him as boy—softness, innocence (literally, *freedom from harm*), passivity, feeling. To become a man is to suffer a wound: we are all Oedipus and Odysseus, moving through life, like each of them, with a limp disguised as a swagger. Through initiation, the boy must effectively die to be reborn as a fully equipped man. The more tradition-bound groups of our culture still have nominal rites that relate to this initiation—brisses and bar mitzvahs, quinces, debutante balls and proms, high school sports and the rest of it. But as our culture has become more fragmented, as belief in a single system of ethical value has disappeared, the process of initiation has also become more fragmented, and its forms have become interestingly complex. They haven't disappeared, they have simply multiplied, becoming ever more invisible as ritual and ever more deeply buried in the traffic of everyday life.

In real life it has been common for hundreds of years—perhaps since the Middle Ages, when medieval businessmen sent their young adult sons, inheritors-to-be of the family business—out on their *Wanderjahre,* times of youthful travel in which the world, encountered as a journey with purposeful stops made along the way, would serve as a sort of living classroom in which the young man, by moving through his journey, would become a certain type of person, would, in fact, be tested by his encounters—like Telemachus—to prove that he was worthy of accepting his father's legacy, manhood itself. In this early modern version of the journey of initiation founded on secular values (the young man is going on the journey ostensibly as his father's business representative—buying and selling, doing the chores of apprenticeship), the young man's challenge is to prove himself or to fail at proving that he is virtuous, most especially that he can be trusted by other men and that he can prove he can take care of himself—in short, that he can be *seen* in the world as a man. Proving you're a man always means, more than anything else, proving yourself to other men.

Again, as the question of value has become more pluralized, so has the sense of what this journey means for the young man. The trope of the journey—an eternal archetype of the search for identity and knowledge—is still very much a part of the ritual of becoming a grown-up, both in real life (in my forties now, I often hear people twenty years my junior talking about going on an extended road trip, backpacking through Europe, and so forth—many of the same things that young men and women of my generation did twenty-five years ago). The initiation journey is, of course, also a persistent trope in works of art. Particularly since World War II, when so many millions of young men left home to fight, and most of whom were then left to try to return to a *sense of home* in a world that had shown to an unprecedented degree the contingency of all human value, the trope of the journey has appeared in ever more problematic, pluralized forms as an expression of the shape the search for self has taken in the world after the Holocaust. In such a world, what must be asked along the journey is often not so much What do I do to become a man? as it is What, if anything, does it mean to *be* a man?

Nowhere has this troubled sense of the search for male identity expressed itself as it has in the road movie. In this film genre which, in my opinion, begins humbly and innocently with the Crosby/Hope *Road to_* movies of the early forties, one can read the growing anxiety about maleness like rings on a tree trunk. While the genre starts as an innocent, silly form of entertainment with the Crosby/Hope series, it soon begins, in films like John Ford's *The Searchers*, to express an ever greater feeling of anxiety about the notion of maleness in a relativized world. Already in *The Searchers* we can see a deep divide forming between different generations of men: it's hard to imagine a Jeffrey Hunter ever turning into a John Wayne (thank goodness!). By the sixties, the road movie has taken the form of *Breathless* and, a little later, *Bonnie and Clyde*. Trouble in paradise.

Discussing the genealogy of the road movie in his book, *A Cinema Without Walls: Movies and Culture After Vietnam*, Timothy Corrigan argues that the road movie is the post-Second World War descendant of the *Bildungsroman*. Like the *Bildungsroman*, Corrigan argues, the road movie treats in a contemporary medium the sentimental education of a young man or, better said, the development of a boy into a man.[1] As a genre concerned with the coming of age of a young man, Corrigan continues, the road movie, evolving in the postwar decade that saw an unprecedented upheaval in the power structures and composition of the family, appears as a genre that is obsessed with defining maleness (and in its later versions, I would add, femaleness[2]) in a time of cultural anxiety.

In early prototypes of the genre, for instance, such as John Ford's *The Searchers* (released in 1956), the narrative is constructed around the central problem of men going on a search for self—that is, for mature manhood—in a journey through a world in which women are present at the periphery of action when they are present at all. The road down which the journey proceeds then becomes a metaphor for the overarching order of patriarchy, which defines the path to true manhood.[3] To err from the road or to be detained, then, is to fail to become a man, just as reaching the end of the road denotes the successful attainment of manhood.

What interests Corrigan as he traces the evolution of the road movie through the fifties, sixties and seventies is the way that, particularly after the end of the Vietnam War (which, like World War II, precipitated mass anxiety about the nature of patriarchy and hence, the nature of maleness), road movies began to depict the search for the male self not as a more or less orderly journey down a road but more and more as an erratic series of detours, as a falling away from the road and hence from gender stereotypes. Citing examples most prominently from the many road movies of Wim Wenders (most of them made in the sixties and seventies), Corrigan concludes that the road movie after Vietnam bends the trope of the successful male journey as expressing self-transformation into a trope of the erratic male journey in which the self is inherently indeterminate.[4]

It is the indeterminacy of the self that is the central concern of Gus Van Sant's road movie, *My Own Private Idaho*. In the story of two young men's search for identity, Van Sant presents the problem of the self's indeterminacy as a multivalently erratic progress. In its visual and aural structure, as well as in the structure of the narratives it develops, the film continually employs the themes and techniques of deviation and error to posit, finally, a sense that the only "truth" that can be discovered in the search for the male self is that such a self is inherently perverse.[5]

The visual structure of *My Own Private Idaho* is perverse in the way the film uses montage to create a sense of continual discontinuity as it develops a narrative. Frequently using jump cuts to move through the story, Van Sant arranges cuts so as to perplex rather than comfortably locate the viewer within a world or a series of logically connected events. For example, the film begins with an image of the definition of the word "narcolepsy" highlighted on the page of a dictionary. As we see this definition of a strange word, we hear, as background music, steel-pedal guitar country music, rich with associations of stereotypical maleness, so that immediately a sense of incongruity is evoked by the film as it juxtaposes a static image of a strange word with the sound of familiar music, creating an effect that is oddly humorous. Then the film cuts to a flat blue screen with the word "Idaho" in its center. Throughout the film, Van Sant uses this same device, a flat colored screen announcing the name of a location, to indicate change of place in the story. The effect is to take an element of movement through the story out of the context of the characters' actions and into that of a mechanical, self-consciously cinematic device. Following this flat, self-conscious image, the film cuts to a scene of a disheveled young man standing in the middle of a country road, returning the viewer to a position inside the film's fictional world only after reminding us that that world is a fiction. If, thus far, we have been located in a cinematic world by these three cuts, our location is nonetheless rendered uncertain: we may be able to figure out that the young man is in Idaho, but the order in which the cuts occur does not permit us to make clear sense of the relationship between the young man, who is in Idaho, and the word "narcolepsy." Several scenes later in the film Van Sant, having introduced the two main characters—Mike, portrayed by River Phoenix, and Scott, portrayed by Keanu Reeves—develops their stories well enough to allow us to feel we have been introduced into a world that defines itself along recognizably conventional, fictional terms. By this point in the film, we have learned that Mike suffers from narcolepsy, while Scott suffers from his father's intense disapproval; we also know, by this point, that Mike and Scott are both street hustlers. Having established these facts, however, Van Sant interrupts the narrative to inject a short series of rapidly cutting, documentary-style monologues delivered by two unidentified young men telling of their first experiences as street hustlers.[6] Since we now know that Mike and Scott are also street hustlers, we can locate these monologues in terms of their connection with the stories of the film's two main characters. What disturbs us about these monologues is that, while being continuous with the rest of the film in terms of content, they undercut the integrity of the fictional world the film has established by juxtaposing the sudden introduction of a sense of the film as reported fact (the monologues) against the structure of the film as constructed fiction (Scott's and Mike's stories). The film further perverts its visual style by cutting rapidly from one scene to another seemingly unrelated scene by presenting two sex scenes as tableaux vivants (the orgy involving Mike, Scott, and the German mechanic, Hans, as well as the sex scene between Scott and his Italian girlfriend), and by injecting several very self-consciously stagy fragments from Shakespeare's *Henry the Fourth*.[7] Taken as a whole, these devices tend to create a broken, discontinuous visual style that continually perverts any sense of narrative or visual coherence.[8]

If the visual style of the film is perverse, so also is the nature of the film's principal characters and their stories. Scott and Mike complement each other in the ways that their individual searches for self, their individual journeys, proceed as a series of errors and detours. What distinguishes Scott from Mike is that while Scott errs intentionally to find himself, Mike's errantry in the process of finding himself is not conscious, but rather the result of being acted upon by the world outside the sphere of his own intention. What finally binds these two characters together is a sense the film gives us that the specifically male identity that both characters are searching for is the sum of all their errors, a polymorphously perverse Other that is always other than itself.

Mike is the central character of the film, but before discussing how Van Sant presents him, it makes sense to discuss his "significant other" in the film, Scott. At the point we meet him, this young man from a wealthy family is about to turn twenty-one. His relationship with his father is troubled: through a few asides he makes, we learn that he feels overburdened by his father's demands that he demonstrate he is ready to accept the mantle of mature manhood. While the father sees his son as being a pervert in the most conventional sense of the word, Scott tells the viewer directly through soliloquies that he sees himself as needing to appear in this light before his father so that, when he reaches his majority, he can surprise his father by shedding his effeminate, youthful self and assert his "manhood." Thus Scott can only prove himself to his father by first appearing to disappoint him: he can only win by appearing first to err.

Having framed this strategy as the central problem for Scott's character, Van Sant adds another level to the perversity that describes Scott's progress by injecting into Scott's story fragments of texts that are alien to the rest of the world of the film: Shakespeare's *Henry the Fourth Parts One* and *Two* and briefly, *Henry the Fifth*.[9] Needless to say, the sections of Scott's story that refer to Shakespeare are stylistically different from the rest of the film. While Van Sant takes liberties with some of Shakespeare's lines (such as the scene in which Scott wakens his sometime mentor Bob, the Falstaff of the film[10]), he clearly directs his actors to perform those lines in a way that is overtly histrionic. The dialogue of the film not taken from Shakespeare is, by contrast, conventionally naturalistic: some of the actors in the film are, in fact, as noted above, untutored nonprofessionals, real street kids; and, as we have noted earlier, one section of the film adopts the opposite of histrionic style, namely, that of documentary reportage. By making Scott's performance as Prince Hal so openly literary, Van Sant sets it at an ironic distance from the naturalistic world of the other sections of the film. Rather than rendering the film completely incoherent, however, the inclusion of the fragments from Shakespeare reinforces the sense that Van Sant is juxtaposing these three performance styles to create a world that is, by nature, disjointed. The different performance styles function as markedly different visual and dramatic textures which, juxtaposed against each other, form a coherent gestalt in the world of the film: the film's world is constituted of fragments, visual and dramatic shards.

There is yet another way in which Scott's resemblance to Prince Hal suggests a kind of perversity or erring in the film. Comparing the Prince Hal scenes in the film with those in Shakespeare, we detect several remarkable contrasts. First, Scott differs from Prince Hal in that he stands to inherit not a kingdom, but a relatively small sphere of local influence. Scott is an ironic character as Northrop Frye uses the term[11]: his transformation is from being a young *roué* to becoming merely a normal guy; whereas Shakespeare's Prince Hal is, arguably, what Frye defines as a high mimetic[12] character who transforms himself from a troubled prince to a heroic monarch. Second, Scott's conflict with his father contrasts with that between Prince Hal and King Henry in that where the latter ends with the father blessing the son and naming him his successor, Scott remains unreconciled with his father. In an important sense, Scott becomes a man while losing his father or, more precisely, after having destroyed him,[13] whereas Prince Hal becomes a man amidst the glow of his father's benediction. Third, while Prince Hal wins a French princess and a significantly enlarged kingdom, Scott attains a badge of conventional manhood by marrying an Italian peasant girl. And finally, while Prince Hal ends his relationship with Falstaff by firmly inviting him to give up his life of vice and join the new order of patriarchal power, Scott's relationship with Bob ends ambiguously. Even after his death, Bob continues to survive as a presence beckoning Scott back to the street life.[14]

When we last see Scott close to the end of the film, he is attending his father's funeral as the Armani-suited, entourage-accompanied, fully recognized head of a conventional patriarchal pack: he is the legitimate heir to his father's legacy. Off in the distance, however, the band of hustlers who had been his confederates, Bob's "children," conduct a noisy, orgiastic celebration over Bob's simple pauper's pine box, which is not buried, but lying on the ground like a Dionysian altar. As the polite funeral of Scott's father proceeds, the street boys begin to taunt Scott by yelling, "Bob! Bob! Bob!" and we see Mike, joining in the noisy disruption, looking with the pain of betrayal and abandonment in Scott's direction. As the camera cuts to a close-up of Scott's face, we see his empty, vaguely smiling face form the centerpiece to the dark scene of the death of the father, until the camera finally cuts to reveal the colorful, kinetic pandemonium of the band of street kids kissing and fondling each other on top of and around Bob's casket. Seeing Scott at the ceremony marking his arrival at the end of his journey, we are left with the sense that, although his search for self has ended with the entombment of his old identity, the self that he has discarded refuses to be buried. Scott has come to bury and replace his father, but the man he has earlier called his true father, Bob, who has also died, lies above ground, and continues at the end to call Scott to err from the path he has chosen. This implies that every aspect of Scott's progress involves erring, both seeking to establish his "true" self (which is a false self) and denying his discarded self (which, in the burial scene, is valued as being his more authentic self). Scott's new, manufactured self thus discovers to the viewer the truth that he is, consummately, perverse; that is, that he is who he is not and he is not who he is.

The chief effect of Scott's story in the film is to serve as a diversion from the film's principal narrative, which is the enigmatic story of Mike's attempt to reclaim his past, find his mother and find a home.[15] It is Mike's story that begins and ends the film: just as, at the beginning of the film, we see Mike standing on a road in the middle of nowhere, at the end of the film we find him in exactly the same place, in exactly the same inexplicable predicament, homeless and headed towards an uncertain destination. Throughout the film, Mike proceeds along his search, his road, by failing, by erring and by following false clues, only to arrive again and again at the same point in the road, the place that looks, as Mike says, "like a fucked-up face." This point in Mike's road comes finally to signify all that can possibly be said or, better yet, all that can be known of his identity, his home.

In the first half hour of the film, Van Sant establishes that Mike and his journey form the central narrative line of the film. Throughout most of the film, the camera looks both at and through his "narcoleptic eyes."[16] When, for instance, we first see Mike fall down in a narcoleptic seizure, the camera reveals his dreams, which appear self-reflexively as home-movie images of the mother and home he has lost and cannot get back. As Harvey Greenberg has noted of this and other scenes involving Mike's seizures, the technique Van Sant has chosen to construct them makes us as viewer continually uncertain whether we are looking at the world of the film from inside or from outside Mike's own mind, so that, as we witness the process of Mike's falling into and out of consciousness, we follow him uncertainly and "recurrently awaken with Mike as if the world were newly invented, under clouded circumstance in obscure locales."[17] Having been introduced to Mike in this way, we next see him in the throes of another seizure while being fellated by one of his regular customers (which provides an ironic counterpoint to Scott's giving up being a hustler and becoming a "regular guy"). As he reaches orgasm, the camera cuts from his contorting ("fucked-up") face to an inexplicable but humorous image of a shack falling out of the sky. The image of the empty shack, the lost and empty home, appears at several other points in the film as the equivalent of reaction shots to suggest Mike's feeling of having lost or being without a home. The additional touch of showing a falling house, of course, calls to mind *The Wizard of Oz,* the idea that "we're not in Kansas anymore" and that "there's no place like home." Mike is, so to speak, one of Dorothy's friends (slang for being gay) and, like Dorothy, he appears before us having been *blown* to a very strange place. It is this strange place, however, that will finally prove to *be* Mike's home: his home is being homeless.

In another early scene showing Mike looking around in the house of a female client, we see him pick up a seashell, and when he holds it to his ears, we hear the plangent roar of waves and the tinkle of a child's music box. However, when shortly afterwards we see the client pick up the shell, we hear nothing. Through such devices the camera is being deeply linked with Mike's subjectivity.

The first part of the film brings to mind other road movies in which, as Corrigan says, the protagonist's progress through time and space occurs as a result largely of events acting upon him[18] rather than as a result of anything the viewer can see as being his intention. Frequently in the film, as noted above, Mike goes from one place to another as a result of having had a seizure and then been being taken somewhere by someone else. At those points in the film in which he does intend to go somewhere, it is always using a clue he has come upon by accident, a clue which, he believes, tells him where to find his mother. But the clues inevitably lead to a cold trail, so that we never see Mike find his mother, and we never see him and his mother together except in the fragments of memory that appear as the "home movie" images he sees when he is unconscious. Whether he arrives at his destination in an unconscious condition or as the result of conscious planning, instead of finding his mother, he finds himself in a strange place with no reason for remaining there.

At two points along the way, Mike's search takes him off the road and by doing so, establishes the perverse nature of his identity as a man. In the scene in which Scott and Mike set out on a stolen motorcycle to visit Mike's brother (in search of clues as to the whereabouts of Mike's mother), Scott and Mike break down at the point in the road with which Mike identifies, the point to which he continually returns: the place with the "fucked-up" face. As they settle down for the night, Mike opens up with great difficulty and, after observing that he might have been normal if he had had a real home, confesses to Scott that he loves him and that he wants to have a sexual kind of closeness with him. Protesting that two men can't love each other (and thereby contradicting his earlier admission that he loves Bob, a pedophile, more than he loves his own father), Scott finally acquiesces and makes love with Mike. Shortly after this union, Scott and Mike get back on the road, which they follow until they come to Mike's brother's house. At this second stop off the road, Mike queries his brother about their mother and learns her supposed present address but ends the visit by quarreling with his brother and revealing to Scott and to the audience that his brother is also his father. At these two way stations, then, Mike reveals the perverse nature of his maleness: he has become the lover of a man who does not believe men can love each other (and who, later in the film, will betray him), and he has revealed the perverse character of his male parentage.

Given these observations about Mike's journey, and given the way Van Sant cuts from Mike's story to Scott's and then, at the end of the film back to Mike again, we can see that Mike's story is perverse in several ways. As we see him err from place to place, we learn that he is perverse in that he is "sick" with narcolepsy, "sick" in his unmanly conduct, and "sick" in his lineage. His journey, defined at the beginning and the end of the film in the image of finding himself repeatedly stuck at the same point on a road in the middle of nowhere, is a perversely described circle in which arriving at the point at which he had begun neither allows him to know the place for the first time nor gives him any closure in his search. Indeed, in the last scene of the film, Mike, having inexplicably returned to "his" place in the road, again falls down in a seizure and is robbed of his shoes by two vindictive strangers. Shortly after the strangers leave him, however, another car pulls up[19] and, in a sequence shot from too great a distance to enable the viewer to identify the second car's driver, we see Mike being picked up, placed in the car, and driven away to an uncertain future. As this scene ends, the film then ends with the words "Have a nice day" displayed against the film's final rendition, again on steel guitar, of "Home of the Brave." The film's final "image," implied in the slogan, is the smiling face, the face of the road, the "fucked-up" inscrutable "face" of Mike's story. By the film's end, we as viewers are left to imagine that the shape of Mike's journey is fixed only in that it seems bound by the road that leads never homeward but always back to the middle of nowhere.

Mike is rarely aware in his world as to where he is; the one place he seems most distinctly to recognize and to identify with is the place in the road with the "fucked-up" face. Similarly, Scott, when we last see him, is unaware that the end of the road for him is the deconstruction of his own journey. What the film seems to offer most clearly in the way of awareness is the recognition in the mind of the audience that the journeys we have seen here are not journeys that lead to a conclusion but journeys that define themselves as a continual detour. It is, at last, this detour that names the Self in the film, for the Self is perverse.

Perversion is openly announced in gregg araki's film *The Living End*, released in 1992.[20] The film opens with credits announcing "an irresponsible film" written and directed by araki (araki prefers his name to be spelled without caps). As the credits roll, we hear the hard, driving rhythm of techno-punk music, and the camera shows as its first images a young, porno-handsome man smirking after having written "Fuck the world" on a wall. As the music continues, the young man dances against a barren landscape. Then he begins to whirl in time with the music, and the camera follows his motion to reveal that he is not in a desert, but rather on the edge of a city—Los Angeles. Facing towards the city, he hurls the can of spray paint he has just used towards it. The camera then pauses to show him from the rear as he faces the city he has just "defaced."

The camera then cuts to black and shows another young man sitting in a car: his expression is one of exasperation and hesitation. As he starts to drive away, the camera reveals the back of his car, where a bumper sticker reading "Choose death" is affixed. As he continues to drive, the camera cuts to black and then he is seen as he drives and makes an entry into his daily journal by microcassette. As he speaks into his recorder, he recounts the mundane details of "just another day," "the first day of the rest" of his life: he has bought a new compact disc and he has found out that he tests positive to the AIDS virus anti-body.

Thus are the two principal characters of the film introduced: Luke (portrayed by Mike Dytri), the graffiti artist, hustler, and outlaw; and Jon (portrayed by Craig Gilmore), the (legitimate) magazine writer and law-abiding citizen. What binds these two men together, we soon learn, is that they are both HIV-positive gay men, each of them dealing in his own way with the implications of having become a diseased pariah. The film follows the two men as their lives first intersect and finally become linked in a frantic psychological and physical journey.

Like *My Own Private Idaho*, araki's film is a road movie. The action of araki's film begins at the edge of two separate roads on which two people begin their progress through experience and towards each other. Using a method of rapid cutting that recalls the discontinuity of Van Sant's film, araki describes the progress of his characters using a visual style that echoes the fragmentation into which their lives have fallen when we meet them. Just as Jon and Luke's story proceeds as a journey that begins and then continues along a meandering road, the film creates a visual sense of the erring quality of their journey by present-ing action as a series of visual blocks linked by interstices of an empty, black screen.

The journey these two men take develops as a series of accidents by means of which they first cross paths by happenstance and then are thrown together by necessity. After we see the two characters introduced separately, we follow their paths in a series of rapidly cut scenes that, at first, do not yield any clear connection (which recalls the discontinuity employed by Van Sant). On the one hand, we follow Luke, in the first section of the film, as he engages in a series of ludicrous brushes with death. He appears to be an aimless drifter—a street-wise picaro—as he hitchhikes, finding along the way a series of lunatics. He first meets a couple of thrill-seeking lesbians who threaten to kill him. Luke manages to turn this situation to his advantage when the two hapless, would-be killers suddenly turn their attention away from him and towards each other, making it possible for him to steal their car and the gun they had intended to use to kill him. He then meets a male trick who picks him up along the road, takes him home for a session of kinky sex, and who then is murdered by the jealous woman lover who suddenly walks in and finds the two men *in flagrante delicto*. Finally, he meets a group of fag-bashers who run into Luke in a city street at night. Again Luke turns the table on his would-be assailants, pulling the stolen gun on them, turning them into pitiably pleading victims as he mercilessly kills them.

In all three of these encounters, the brush with danger is played for camp value, played in the manner of an early John Waters movie: the lesbians lose Luke by bickering ridiculously between themselves; the jealous lover, who looks like a character out of *Pink Flamingoes* or *Female Trouble*, kills her lover while ignoring Luke, which again allows him to escape rather improbably from danger; and the fag-bashers, shown at first as a band of swaggering, smugly confident bullies, are reduced to a group of whimpering boys who have gotten in over their heads but who are not likely to win the sympathy of gay viewers, to whom the film is primarily addressed. The net result of these three scenes is to heighten the viewer's sense that, although Luke may be a criminal, he has been driven to his crimes by circumstances beyond his control: the world around him is crazy, and his perverse behavior is aimed only at surviving in such a world.[21] By playing the violence as camp, araki engages his gay audience to experience anger from a distinctly queer point of view: the real violence here consists more in how the images of Luke's opponents appear than in what happens to them. All of Luke's adversaries are caricatures, and in these three episodes, he stands out among them as the only real human being we see.

Cutting between Luke's three encounters with the ridiculous[22] are scenes of Jon, the upright young man, trying to cope with his anxiety about his HIV status. Juxtaposed against the campy scenes of violence involving Luke are scenes of Jon as he drives, in silent exasperation, and as he gives the bad news to his good friend Darcy. Shot in a very sickly light and using mostly the low camera angle that predominates throughout the film, the scene of Jon and Darcy holding on to each other in the living room of Darcy's apartment is awkward, unpleasant, and full of unresolved emotion. In fact, the scene is so expertly disappointing that the viewer watching it might be inclined to feel uncomfortably implicated as a voyeur. The low camera angle and the awkwardness of the performances give us the impression we're watching a hidden camera video, peeking into someone else's life. What we see looks painfully unrehearsed, ironically true to life: Jon and Darcy holding each other uneasily, Darcy blaming one of Jon's slut-boyfriends for giving him the disease of the century, and, most painful of all, Jon ending up spending too much time giving comfort to Darcy when it is she to whom he has come for help.

As we see Jon driving again, he (almost literally) runs into Luke just after Luke has gunned down the fag-bashers. Luke runs into Jon's car brandishing a gun, and the surprised Jon stops just long enough to give Luke an opportunity to jump into the car and demand that he keep driving. Thus begins their very odd relationship: Jon is aimlessly running from his bad news, and Luke is running from his. The two collide in an erring path of desperation that throws them into each other's lives. Their meeting appears finally as a blend of accident and necessity, unpredictability and inevitability. In the odd world this film has constructed, these two boys seem made for each other.

Because of the way araki sets up Jon and Luke's individual narratives, we are led to see the road as a metaphor for their individual emotional states and histories: as we meet them, both men are going nowhere along a path on which they cannot seem to find what they deeply need. When Jon picks up Luke, he asks him where he wants to go; Luke responds that he would like to leave "this insane planet." Jon's question and Luke's childish, sociopathic answer give us the roadmap their journey will follow for the rest of the film: Jon is looking for someone to show him a way out, and Luke's "plan" is simply to keep going, despite everything.

I think it is central to the film that both of the main characters are writers of a sort: Jon, as we find him, has already come to the end of his pretensions as a serious academic. Even he no longer believes in his own attempts to inscribe himself upon the intellectual landscape for which his education and his sensibilities have prepared him. Thus, when Jon speaks of his work as a writer, he talks sheepishly about his work on "The Death of the Cinema," no doubt a cutting-edge piece of academic hack work drawn from the liturgy of metatheory. Luke is also a writer, but one of the more visceral sort—a wandering graffiti artist who leaves the traces of his own rootlessness as he wanders about in a world he believes has been ruined for the young by the previous generation. Jon is the tired intellectual who does not believe in what he is doing with his life, and Luke is the carefree nihilist who believes all that is left for him is to keep giving the world a piece of his mind. Framing their characters against the different types of writing they perform, araki sets the two men up as essentially two different voices—queer ones—talking back to AIDS. Jon's voice is formal, weak, passive, emptied out, deconstructed, and Luke's is irrational, active, rather pleased with itself, and focused on defiance.

When it becomes apparent that the two men must get out of town—Luke, it seems, has shot a cop and Jon is just about to come out of his skin over the whole mess of his life—it is Luke who takes charge, quickly energizing Jon, at least for a time, and urging him to do *something*. What follows for the rest of the film is a meandering road trip in which Jon and Luke drive, mostly at night, commit a series of petty crimes (credit card fraud, defacing instant teller machines) and not-so-petty ones. The latter consist of Jon and Luke's re-exposing each other to the AIDS virus by having unsafe sex with each other in the sleazy hotels and roadside stops along their way. Paradoxically, having unsafe sex is both a crime they commit together—they both realize the implications of exposing themselves repeatedly to the virus—and a statement of their growing commitment to one another. The longer Jon is exposed to Luke's influence, the more Jon is able to stop caring about the consequences of his actions or about the future. At least for a while during the journey, he is able to focus instead on the mad passion that Luke offers him. But Jon's decision to give in to his unsafe sexual urges is made believable by the fact that, from the very beginning of the film, araki has made Luke appear both to Jon and to the audience conversant in gay male sexual imagery as a stunning embodiment of the gay male stereotype of the perfect hunk, an antidote to the death of the flesh that is the promise of AIDS:

> ... cool Luke, a James Dean *manqué*, taunts Jon with a 'live young, die young and leave a beautiful corpse' credo. With his bare torso, his fashionably ragged jeans and cigarette hanging from his mouth, he represents the homoerotic ideal of hard masculinity .... The libidinous Luke endows [Jon and his] relationship with a remarkable charge.[23]

As we see Jon begin to loosen up psychologically under Luke's sociopathic influence, becoming ever more deeply implicated in Luke's pattern of crime, we also see Jon begin to find some sense of relief from his own pain, so that, as Jon himself begins to act out more sociopathically, he also seems to become more alive. Whereas at the beginning of the film he alternately displays tension and resigned passivity both in his actions and in his voice, Jon, as he becomes more deeply influenced by Luke, becomes, at least briefly, more energetic and more expressive. Paradoxically, the more Jon exposes himself, through Luke, to death, the more alive he appears to be. Araki seems to imply that, because both men are homosexual and HIV positive, the world around them has forced them to flee any received sense of what it means to live within the law.[24] It is at this point that we understand the two men have become linked in a decision that will demand their embarking upon a journey that, clearly for us as viewers as well as for them as active characters, *must* proceed just as certainly as it *must* lead to an outside, a place beyond what the world has so far allowed them to be.

Jon and Luke's journey doesn't wind up leading them anywhere; in a sense, the where of their journey's end is *nowhere*. After several mishaps and a botched suicide attempt, the two men wind up off the road altogether, on a beach, facing the ocean as they sit in exhaustion. In a beautiful, sad image that shows the two men as tiny figures facing a great gray expanse of rushing water, the film seems to leave us with a metaphor for the condition of gay men and people with HIV in a society that, even after over fifteen years of "facing" the AIDS crisis, is overwhelmingly homophobic and AIDS-phobic. If men in Jon and Luke's condition are hopelessly beyond both medicine and the law, they are, nonetheless, not hopeless. After all, they are together at the end of the film as they face the indifferent ocean. Having veered off the road of polite society, they gain access to a truth that the rest of the world cannot know. They can see where they are, they can even hear the sound of being nowhere. As the lone human presence at the end of the film, then, Jon and Luke present something of the feeling of being diseased gay pariahs: the knowledge they have gained along the road, their consciousness of being gay men who have fought, hurt and loved each other, has brought them together but has separated them from the rest of the world. Criminal outcasts, Jon and Luke survive as the film's final human presence, while what remains of the culture that has cast them off is the image of vast, powerful, but undifferentiated and unconscious mass.[25]

What araki has done in *The Living End* is turn an old cinematic stereotype on its head: in this film, the homosexual as monstrous felon is not presented to make a case for society's censure of the homosexual but rather to make a case for gay people to become actively, angrily involved in fighting for their lives.[26] That the film announces itself from the beginning as being "an irresponsible film" is an acknowledgment by araki that something of what he presents in the film is, in a sense, wrong. To suggest that two men could get away with a rather serious crime spree is wrong; to suggest that two men who love each other should engage in possibly life-threatening sex is wrong; to suggest that the culture in which we live is chock-full of violent, sex-driven lunatics is wrong; and to suggest that the culture in which we live is as indifferent to us as the ocean is, perhaps, also wrong. It is the very extreme images through which this film presents what is wrong that provide a space for reading the film not as a rationalization for criminality but rather as a passionate plea for people to act in defense of treating homosexuals with decency.

Technically, the film sets up a visual structure that plays with "wrongness" in a number of ways. First, araki succeeds, whether by intention or by accident, in giving the film a "wrong" look by directing some of his characters to act very histrionically, while others (chiefly Jon and Luke) act as if they learned acting in a different universe. For example, the scene in which Luke is taunted by the two killer lesbians employs a ridiculously amateurish acting style. In this scene, as the two killer lesbians—Daisy and Fern—fight jealously, Fern accuses Daisy of wanting to have sex with Luke. As she rails at Daisy, Fern delivers a catalogue of vulgar synonyms for "penis" that, in its delivery as in its imagery, childishly undercuts what would otherwise be the considerable tension present in a scene of two women holding a gun on a strange man. Later, when Luke is discovered in bed with the man who picks him up, the distraught lover, dressed, as I've already commented, in over-the-top sixties camp clothing and garish makeup, emotes in the manner of a drag queen in a mad romp. When the woman pulls a butcher knife out of her purse, the parody of violence in the scene reaches a higher level, which finally goes over into slasher-movie silliness when we see a close-up of the dead man's dog licking the blood off his lifeless arm. Throughout the film, couples appear on the street in bondage and discipline garb (the woman leading the man by a dog chain), crazily reciting the Preamble to the Constitution in a convenience store parking lot, or, in the case of Darcy and her boyfriend, arguing over whether Jon's taste for morbid music (Joy Division, Dead Can Dance) is part of what caused him to get this AIDS thing. Virtually all the characters in the film except Jon and Luke are presented as histrionic stereotypes, while Jon and Luke themselves are presented as having a good deal of emotional depth. Virtually all of the many close-up shots in the film are images of Jon and Luke, and it is in Jon and Luke, primarily, that we see what looks like real tenderness.

The film also uses a number of "wrong" visual devices. One such device is the film's frequent cuts to a black screen briefly between scenes. This device, which serves to present cuts in time and space from scene to scene, functions as a *Verfremdungseffekt* to remind us that we are watching a film. Another reminder is araki's use of consistently low camera angles: rather a bit too often the film seems to be shot at crotch level, which encourages the viewer to look at the whole story from a naughty point of view[27] and which, as a matter of cinematic style, tends to foreground the film's point of view as being not Hollywood, as being outlaw. Color in the film is very pale: interior shots have a bilious, neon-lit quality, and the few daylight exterior scenes are bleached into an intensely pale, glaring light. Much of the film is shot at night, especially the scenes in which Jon and Luke are driving. These scenes, full of shadow and silvery light, suggest both the intimacy of Jon and Luke's getting to know one another and the difficulty for the viewer of seeing what Jon and Luke see.

Yet another visual device that araki uses connects with one of the film's dramatic themes: the presence and function of language. Throughout their road trip, Jon and Luke stop beside monumental road signs that bespeak the pleasures of traveling: car dealership signs depicting giant cowboys, convenience store signs, bank signs and motel signs. When the camera pauses on these signs, we get a sense of how empty of meaning they are.[28] When, for instance, Jon and Luke pause under the sign of a giant, grinning cowboy, they are tired and at odds with each other; when they pause to get money at an instant teller machine, the machine is broken (and Luke blows it away with his stolen gun); when Luke steals the car of the lesbians who have just threatened to kill him, the camera pulls back to reveal a bumper sticker on the back of the car that reads "I love Jesus." Often in the film, it seems, commercial(ized) signs function as cinematic signs indicating that Jon and Luke are at odds with the culture at large, that the culture's language is not theirs.

Clearly, the most significant presentation of wrongdoing depicted or implied in the film is the depiction of Jon and (primarily) Luke's crimes. Jon is an accessory, having been drawn into crime by Luke, who provides him with relief from his anxiety at learning he is infected. Jon becomes an active participant in lawless behavior, however, when he agrees to have unprotected sex with Luke. But again, it is Luke who asks him to do this as a proof that each man cares for the other more than he cares for life. Thus Jon's criminal act of unprotected sex is mitigated by the fact that it is an attempt to ignore his bond with society in favor of his bond with Luke. Luke's crimes are also mitigated by his sense that the world through which he wanders is peopled by hostile crazies whom he has to fight. In the logic of the film, the people with whom Luke fights are less than he is: they are parodies of hunger and sentiment who are no match for his raw, lively passion.

A number of contrasts present themselves between Van Sant's and araki's films. First, it seems clear that araki's film is more specifically directed at gay audiences than is Van Sant's. *The Living End* announces itself, both at the beginning and end of the film, as a gesture of radical queer politics. Araki specifically dedicates the film to the people who have died and are yet to die from AIDS as a result, araki says in less polite terms, of government indifference. As such, araki's outrageous presentation of gay criminals as heroes is meant both to arouse the silent majority of gay men and lesbians to decisive actions to protect themselves and to warn those on the other side of the aisle that gay men are capable of striking back at anyone who pisses them off. Van Sant's film, by contrast, is political only in a more covert sense. To the extent that it valorizes being gay and places heterosexuality in brackets, *My Own Private Idaho* is implicitly political in that it affirms what the status quo would deny about sexual identity and about patriarchy. In a greater sense, however, Van Sant's film is more a postmodernist work about gen-x ontology than it is a polemic criticizing social relationships. In Van Sant's film, Mike's embracing gayness and Scott's denying it are significant but finally subordinate values in the primary project of the film, which is not to speak for gay people but rather to speak about all people. As noted above, Van Sant himself sees that the film encourages the audience to identify with Mike, particularly in the matter of how Mike's story continues after the film ends. Because the film succeeds so well in allowing the audience to go inside Mike's head (which araki's film never attempts to do with his characters) and considering Van Sant's statements, it seems clear that the film is meant to invite the audience to extrapolate from what they have learned about Mike not only to figure out what will happen to him but also how his condition speaks to theirs. Because Mike's character is constructed as arising out of a set of conditions, the audience's identification with him thus serves not as a call to action (as with araki), but to the recognition that Mike's life is the (postmodernist) audience's life: we are all homeless, we are all perverse.

What ties *My Own Private Idaho* together with *The Living End* is the way both films use the conventional genre of the road movie to explore what it means to be a gay man moving about in a hostile culture. In both films, the journey is portrayed as a series of accidents and detours, metaphors for the gay man's deviations from the "straight" (and narrow) order defined by heterosexist patriarchy. In neither film does the journey lead to a conclusion. Scott and Mike never arrive anywhere, anywhere that can be considered *their* destination, their *true* home, their fixed place in the world. Similarly, Jon and Luke arrive nowhere but at the edge of a nameless road, and if they have a home, it is with each other, matched up against the vastness of the ocean.

Both films refer to the precariousness of gay men's position in society. In an earlier generation of films depicting gay men (such as, for instance, William Friedkin's adaptation of Mart Crowley's *The Boys in the Band*) uncertainty, vagrancy, the whole condition of being an outcast, tend to signify that gay men are inherently, fatally vulnerable people. This vulnerability arises directly from the fact that gay men, *before Stonewall*, are usually constructed as being, above all else, constitutionally unable to integrate themselves into "normal" society.

Mart Crowley's gay men, most of whom cannot even "pass" for straight, are condemned to perform an endlessly repeating simulation of normal social life— friendship, intimacy, honesty, passion—that almost always gives way to the social "truth" lying underneath. This "truth" is that, finally admitting the monstrous nature of each other's sexuality, these men must continually turn on each other and themselves, thereby completing the attack that their mere existence has conducted against the legitimate social order. Born assaulting that order, they inevitably assault themselves, and thus concludes their story.

Van Sant appropriates the condition of gay men's social vulnerability not to define social pathology, but to affirm character positively. Mike's narcolepsy is a natural condition, a condition that commands and also sustains him. The seizures into which he falls serve to protect him (from the pain of separation from home and mother) and, for a time, to return him to that home and to her. It is also through the seizures that he returns, throughout the film, to Scott, his true love, and to his special place in the road which, as recurring center of action in the film, is also Mike's "center." If Mike's action is always erring, it is also, nonetheless, inexorably oriented about a point in space. That point in space, Mike's place in the road, *is* nowhere because it *is* outside the order of patriarchal society (just as Mike's patriarchy is). In a very real sense, then, Mike's narcolepsy (physical monstrosity), his homosexuality and his homelessness (social monstrosity) mark him as being the film's most authentic character: unlike Scott, Mike is always, of necessity, true to his condition and his place. Because Mike's monstrosity is presented as being more authentic than Scott's attainment of normalcy, it is the conventionally conceived monstrous character in the film who ends up embodying a character that is affirmative.

By contrast, the perverse Oedipal drama enacted by Scott serves to indict the "normalcy" of heterosexuality: in Scott it is the heterosexual, patriarchal persona that is false, a deformation of the authentic identity that he comes to deny, even as his life as a street hustler continues to call to him. To attain his new identity, or rather, to manufacture it, Scott has destroyed his biological father and has denied the paternity of the man he has earlier referred to as his "true" father (Bob). It is significant that, in the scene in which Scott witnesses his biological father's burial, Scott stands silently while, off in the distance, the band of hustlers yells Bob's name repeatedly: it is the name of the "true" yet denied father that is passionately spoken, not the name of the "murdered" one. In the last analysis, all that is affirmative in Mike is denied in Scott: unlike Mike, who is presented as having a condition over which he has no control, Scott is presented as a character who controls everything both within and around himself but to no real avail; where Mike announces affirmatively the perverse nature of his parentage, Scott silently denies his own perverse parentage; where Mike finally proves (for the viewer) to be true to himself by being carried away at the end of the film, Scott, in the end, proves that he has been untrue by assuming a fixed position (his father's legacy). Perhaps most significant for the film is the way that Van Sant chooses to conclude Mike's and

Scott's stories: whereas Mike's story is presented with a manifestly open ending, with Mike going off into the unknown, Scott's is presented as ending amid the threat that what he has made of himself will soon unravel. At the end of this film, it is the social monster who is in a state of creative equilibrium; it is the straight boy who is about to come apart at the seams.

Conversely, araki constructs the social vulnerability and monstrosity of gay men as being affirmative for his gay characters. Luke and Jon are both extraordinarily handsome: the sensual power they display as they make love plays easily and fiercely, which affirms unequivocally for the audience that the sexual energy of their being gay is something that does not ask to be explained or apologized for. More overtly sexual than Van Sant's film, araki's film attacks the notion that gay sexuality is monstrous by depicting it, straightforwardly and believably, as being beautiful and intense, and fuck you if you're not ready for it.

The monstrousness of Luke's crimes is presented as being not only understandable but almost virtuous: his opponents are all laughable figures—killer lesbians, the wife of a two-timing bisexual, a gang of bullies—who would probably have ended up badly even without his help. Similarly, Jon's abandonment of his legitimate life in favor of a life of crime with Luke looks, in the balance, like something of an improvement: no more articles on "The Death of the Cinema," no more pet goldfish to worry about. In Jon's brief adventure with Luke, we might suspect, there is more substance than there was in much of his life before. And finally, araki's gay men, monsters that they are, prove to have a more stable relationship than do the other characters of the film—where Darcy breaks off her relationship with her boyfriend because she learns that he has been untrue to her, Luke and Jon, despite their problems, remain together.

Again, the vulnerability that araki's characters display at the end of the film ends up affirming rather than discrediting gay sexuality. Here vulnerability represents a final openness between Jon and Luke: no longer fighting or cajoling Jon, Luke is finally *with* him. While we do not know what will happen next with Jon and Luke, we know that for them, as for Mike in Van Sant's film, the story is not yet over.

NOTES

1. Timothy Corrigan, *A Cinema Without Walls: Movies and Culture After Vietnam* (New Brunswick, N.J.: Rutgers University Press, 1991), 143-44.

2. It is significant that Corrigan's study, first published in 1991, appeared before *Thelma and Louise* (Dir. Ridley Scott, 1992) was released. If a central part of Corrigan's thesis about road movies is the contention that the road symbolizes the "straight and narrow" path of patriarchal order, the question then arises whether a film such as *Thelma and Louise* can be seen as an instance, for which there are other notable examples (e.g., *Badlands* and *Sugarland Express*, both released in 1974), of the road movie as an explication of the search for

"femaleness." If Corrigan's thesis holds, then it would be consistent to see the journey along the road as a search for sexual identity, male or female, since that search will always be conducted as a response to the law-giving order which, as a matter of political reality, is the order of the father.

3. Corrigan, 144.

4. Corrigan, 153.

5. By "perverse" I mean "erring" in the sense of "not adhering to a single path." This sense of the word "perverse" thus contains a paradox: that of a path which is, by definition, a continuous changing of paths. For a discussion of this sense of the word "perverse," especially as it pertains to contemporary gay culture, see Frank Browning, *The Culture of Desire: Paradox and Perversity in Gay Lives Today* (New York: Crown Publishers, Inc., 1993), particularly chapter 9, "Paradox and Perversity." The present study is also immensely indebted to the discussion of perversity found in Jonathan Dollimore's *Sexual Dissidence: Augustine to Wilde, Freud to Foucault* (Oxford: Clarendon Press), 1992.

6. In a *Rolling Stone* interview with David Handelman, Van Sant discusses the fact that he used several real street hustlers—two of whom deliver the documentary-style monologues—as actors in the film. As a thematic element, then, these monologues are doubly disruptive in the film: they stand outside the rest of the film's action, and they are, indeed, actual accounts of street hustlers' lives. See Handelman, "Gus Van Sant's Northwest Passage," *Rolling Stone*, 31 October 1991, n616: 61.

7. Brian D. Johnson, reviewing Van Sant's film, finds in the histrionic style of the film's Shakespeare fragments a dramatic *flaw*. See Johnson, Review of *My Own Private Idaho*, *Maclean's*, 28 October 1991, v104, n43: 101.

8. Handelman remarks (op. cit., 62) that what holds all the visually "dissonant" elements together is the musical continuity provided by the steel guitar music, centering on variations, recurring throughout the film, of "Home of the Brave." Ascribing an element of continuity to the film's music only serves to underscore the film's perversity: what holds the film together is not a visual element that explicitly links the pieces of stories that the viewer sees, but rather the reiteration of a nonvisual element, music, that plays ironically against those pieces as a form of implicit comment. The implicit comment arises from an ironic distance between the viewer's recognition that the music is about fine, upstanding, regular men singing the praises of home, while the film is about homeless, depraved derelicts.

9. David Hansen, reviewing the film in *Newsweek*, quotes Van Sant as acknowledging his debt to Orson Welles's *Chimes at Midnight* (1966) as being the *primary* source for the film's allusions to Shakespeare. Welles the Hollywood outsider, Ansen reminds us, rewrote Shakespeare to place Falstaff at the center of action in his film (which, like Van Sant's, was produced outside Hollywood and on a shoestring budget). Thus Van Sant, in turning to Welles,

has rewritten Welles's rewriting of Shakespeare. This fact yields yet another sense in which perversion enters into Van Sant's film, for in it he has deliberately "erred" from Welles's "original." See Hansen, "Prince Hal in Portland: the risk-taking director of 'Drugstore Cowboy' makes a bold new movie on his hometown streets" in *Newsweek*, 15 April 1991, v117, n15: 68.

10. Falstaff is portrayed by underground film director William Richert, whose film *Winter Kills* (1979), according to Harvey R. Greenberg, yields yet another filmic reference to Van Sant's film. In *Winter Kills*, according to Greenberg, "the son who ambivalently distances himself from his tycoon father's domination discovers the vile patriarch has connived his other presidential son's execution when the latter became a liberal threat." Also mentioning Van Sant's debt to Welles, Greenberg describes the film as having "wheels within wheels." See Greenberg, Review of *My Own Private Idaho*, *Film Quarterly*, Fall 1992, v46, n1: 24.

11. Northrop Frye, *Anatomy of Criticism* (Princeton, N.J.: Princeton University Press, 1971), 40.

12. Frye, 43.

13. By means of which development the film, with a touch of particularly deft black humor, relates conventional manhood to Oedipal violence. Significantly, the woman with whom Scott consummates his crime of parricide is a foreigner (an Italian *gamine*).

14. No less significant is the fact that William Richert 'survives' as a professional father to Van Sant: Richert, the elder avant-garde filmmaker, is precursor to Van Sant the postmodernist artist.

15. David Ansen, Review of *The Living End*, *Newsweek*, 31 August 1992, v120, n9: 69.

16. Brian D. Johnson, 101.

17. Greenberg, 23.

18. Corrigan, 145.

19. In an interview with Graham Fuller that appears as introduction to the published screenplay of *My Own Private Idaho*, Van Sant comments on the fact that, whereas in the original screenplay it is clear that Scott is the person who rescues Mike, in the film the rescuer's identity is intentionally left uncertain: "You're not supposed to know [who finally picks up Mike or why he does], really. It's like the end of *Drugstore Cowboy*, where people don't know whether Bob dies or survives. Some people have asked me who picks Mike up. In a way, it's either *you* who's the person picking him up or you're *him*, just being asleep. Or it's just a non-ending, and you assume he will go on in his quest. He's a character that has a hard time changing, so he's just going to go on like that forever-wandering and searching." (The emphasis is Van Sant's.) See Graham Fuller, "Gus Van Sant: Swimming Against the Current," in Gus Van Sant, *Even Cowgirls Get the Blues* and *My Own Private Idaho* (Boston: Faber and Faber, 1993), xlv.

20. Reviewing araki's film, David Ansen remarks that araki directed, wrote, shot and edited the film, which cost $23,000 to make. Virtually but not explicitly naming araki as the film's *auteur*, Ansen remarks that araki's labeling his film as "irresponsible" "means that his bold mixture of black, gross-out humor and frank homoeroticism isn't likely to please the Pat Buchanan crowd." This is tantamount to saying that araki is using the film to address both conservatives (with horror) and, more importantly, gay audiences (with indignation). See Ansen, 68.

21. Writing in the *New York Times*, Janet Maslin remarks that "the film's crime spree is presented as an understandable response to AIDS-related rage." See Maslin, review of *The Living End*, *New York Times*, National Edition, 3 April 1992, v141: C-1.

22. In *Sight and Sound*, Lizzie Franke observes in this connection that "araki's movie is almost playfully picaresque. [Jon and Luke] encounter a succession of archetypes *en route* ... pop-up ciphers who are negligible in the final analysis." See Franke, review of *The Living End*, *Sight and Sound*, February 1993, v3, n2: 49.

23. Franke, 50.

24. Franke, 50.

25. Janet Maslin notes that "like *Thelma and Louise* which [araki's film] resembles on a more modest and desperate scale, *The Living End* uses crime as a way of extricating its characters from everyday society, and not as an occasion for passing moral judgment on their behavior. Getting out is what matters, not getting even." See Maslin, C-1.

26. Roy Grundmann, "The fantasies we live by: bad boys in *Swoon* and *The Living End*." *Cineaste*. Fall 1992, XIX, iv: 25.

27. Unless araki, by using a device that is the stock-in-trade of pornography, is implicating the audience in a transgression of the limits between "polite" movie viewing and perverse voyeurism.

28. Janet Maslin, in her review of the film, observes of this use of language in the film that "suddenly, in this film's funhouse universe, even the simplest of platitudes looks mad." See Maslin, C-1.

CHAPTER 3

Jean Cocteau, Kenneth Anger and Jean Genet

For Van Sant and araki, the search for self describes a perverse progress that affirmatively links the monstrous nature of homosexuality with existential authenticity. By positing this link, these two filmmakers subvert the traditional notion of the homosexual as social monster. Presenting homosexuals as outlaws, such films clearly develop a sense that the homosexual criminal can be seen as being more engaging and as being more creatively, fully and actively human, than the "normal" people around him.

By choosing the trope of the road trip to present the argument that establishes a link between criminality and authenticity, Van Sant and araki leave the viewer to consider this link as arising from the fundamental theme that both films share with each other and with road movies in general. This theme is, implicitly, a two-part question: Who are we, and how do we become what we are?

If, in asking about the nature of identity, Van Sant and araki focus, specifically for homosexual characters, on asking how we become what we are, they describe what we might view as being logically the first step for gay filmmakers in uncovering a more fundamental question embedded within that posed by the road movie, namely, What is the nature of homosexual identity?

This second question, What is the nature of homosexual identity, was first addressed by a number of gay filmmakers a good many years before Van Sant and araki appeared to ask questions of their own. Influenced substantially by the work Jean Cocteau did in film and other media during the thirties and forties (particularly *Le sang d'un poète*, released in 1930), Kenneth Anger, in his film *Fireworks* (1947) and Jean Genet, in his film *Un chant d'amour* (English title: *A Song of Love*, made in 1950) created works which presented darkly homoerotic images with a matter-of-factness that even now is striking because it is something we so rarely see in a film. Just as Cocteau's surrealist art film, privately made under the sponsorship of the Vicomte De Noailles, marked an important first step in the presentation of powerful, disturbing, demonic images of the homosexual as creator, as power source, the two films by Anger and Genet appear even fifty years after their making as extraordinary examples of homosexual artists embracing the notion of monstrosity as source of power for identity and for creation.

As of 1925 Jean Cocteau was using opium regularly but had not yet felt the decline that comes from extended use. It was at this time, one of enormous inner turmoil, that he wrote his play *Orphée*, which was conceived ostensibly as a monument to his conversion to Catholicism under the sponsorship of Jacques Maritain.[1] In the play, Cocteau uses the Orpheus myth as a vehicle for his own life story, a story of being first seduced artistically and spiritually by Surrealism, from which shackles he ultimately frees himself when he finds his way back to the one true inspiration, which, in the framework of his play, is the Church. Marking Cocteau's first use of the Orpheus myth in his work, this short play provided some of the basic thematic material that the artist would later articulate much more artfully in his film by the same name. Missing from the film is the Christian Activist sentiment that, owing to its insincerity, mars the play. Indeed, Cocteau's conversion was a disaster, for even while he was visiting the fervently religious Maritain, taking Holy Communion in the latter's home and professing publicly a recanting of the numerous (as well as various) sins of his frivolous past, Cocteau was continuing to smoke opium.

The play *Orphée* was originally conceived as a retelling of the story of Christ. Cocteau's plan for the work changed most drastically and fatefully when, on his way to visit his friend Picasso in 1925, he experienced a hallucination, no doubt brought on at least in part by his drug use. The hallucination occurred while Cocteau was riding an elevator. As the artist tells the story, he heard a voice in the elevator say "My name is on the plate!" and read on the nameplate the word "Heurtebise"; upon returning to the same elevator later, Cocteau noticed the trademark "Otis" on the same plate, and later came to the conclusion that the episode had been an encounter with a creative force he came to identify as being an angel (the name Heurtebise suggested wings beating against a windowpane). Cocteau believed he had been possessed by this angel and that it returned to overcome him to produce his art. Subsequently he composed the poem "L'ange Heurtebise," a deeply homoerotic poem that describes the possession of the poet by an angel/lover. The essence of the poem is Cocteau's vision of the creative process of the artist as a process of becoming; that process is made possible by the intervention of a demonic god/lover, who, by possessing the artist in an experience that fuses the physical and the spiritual, reshapes him with the powers of darkness and erotic surrender.

Somewhat before composing "L'ange Heurtebise" Cocteau had been introduced—by his friend Blaise Cendrars—to the works of Rilke, especially the *Duino Elegies* and the *Sonnets to Orpheus*. Years before that Cocteau and Rilke had even been neighbors in the Hotel Biron in Paris, and though each knew of the other's presence, they never appear to have had much contact. Even so, it appears that Rilke's work had a great impact on Cocteau,[2] whose chief artistic gift may well have been how fully he comprehended and incorporated into his own work the great currents of artistic creativity he found in the world around him. In this connection, it is important to note how close and enduring were Cocteau's associations with other major luminaries of the art world of his time: Guillaume Apollinaire, Igor Stravinski, Sergei Diaghilev, Pablo Picasso, Georges Auric, Coco Chanel and Raymond Radiguet were among his closest associates and were, along with the more distant influence of Rilke's work, critical to the formation of his artistic sensibilities.

Much of what began with the poem "L'ange Heurtebise" and the play *Orphée* speak to the central concept in Cocteau's work, which is the nature of poetry. Reflections on the nature of poetry and the experience of the poet are everywhere in his work, and what interests me here is the way that Cocteau develops his ideas about poetry from his own version of the Orphic myth. When Cocteau speaks of poetry, he understands it in the most ancient sense of the word: the poet is a *maker*; a poem is thus any artifice that partakes of an experience of contact with the Orphic muse. This sense of understanding the process and the work of poetry are important here because they provide something of a signpost that leads Cocteau to making films. Beginning with "L'ange Heurtebise," Cocteau proceeded to compose works that describe how poetry is made and what happens to the poet during the making of the poem. For Cocteau, the whole notion of poetry is to be understood as a process whereby the poet is possessed by a creative force and in the process of this possession dies as an identity. During this death the poet descends into an underworld, like Orpheus, and this death of his identity corresponds with the birth of the poem.

In the introduction to his first film, *Le sang d'un poète* (1930), Cocteau states it is his intention in the work to "photograph poetry" in a "documentary" way. Of his play *Orphée* he once said that it is an attempt to tell "where poems come from." The involuted nature of Cocteau's work—the creation of works of art whose aim is to tell how works of art come into being—comprises the major form of the circular or cyclical conceptualization that recurs throughout his work in many forms, each bearing a unique level of meaning that mirrors the epic cycle of which Orpheus is the prime symbol. From the classical myth of Orpheus, with its plot of the epic heroic journey through the underworld, which results in an emergence that is essentially a rebirth, Cocteau drew the basic material on which he built a philosophy of poetry. The phenomenon of poetry thus explained became for Cocteau a primary principle of existence, and he often spoke of his own life as a work of art. For him, the poet is an intermediary between the world of everyday reality and a more pure form of reality that exists in the "beyond." To the extent that a poet succeeds in conveying a sense of this "beyond," he fulfills his mission as artist. In other words, poetry is what the poet reports on his trip to the underworld. his trip into darkness.

Cocteau began making films at the age of forty. By that time he had published several novels, plays, collections of poetry, journals, criticism and drawings, and he had collaborated with other artists on libretti, oratorios and ballets. Though the quality of his work varied widely and, true to the spirit of his times, inspired a good deal of lively controversy, Cocteau at forty had established himself as an autonomous artistic presence. His first cinematic effort evolved out of a commission from two of his most generous patrons, Charles and Marie-Laure de Noailles. Originally conceived as an animated cartoon, the project quickly became a more personal one in his hands, changing finally into a film that would concern itself with the nature of poetry and which ultimately became *Le sang d'un poète*. In all his previous work Cocteau had never had any contact with film, so that he set out on this first project with no technological knowledge of the medium and with no direction or restriction (outside the budget of one million francs) as to how to execute the project. Choosing his technicians by interview, Cocteau wrote the scenario himself and engaged his friend Georges Auric to compose incidental music for the film. The resulting project was a film that survives as an important first statement of the nature of the Orphic force and experience, and even more important for us here, it survives as a powerful image of queer identity that suggests an equivalence between monstrousness, power and creativity. It appropriates the hermetic visual language of surrealism to present a series of ambiguous, suggestive vignettes that show the angel muse—pictured as a black figure with obviously artificial wings—as he tracks and wounds the poet while the latter wanders through a world of disturbing, erotically charged images. The relationship between artist and muse is really presented as something of a game of cat-and-mouse: the artist is seen looking for the muse, and the muse is seen hunting down the artist. What interests me about this film is the fact that it presents one of the earliest, extensively articulated visual statements that presents an equation between darkness, homoerotic desire, and individual power. As such it is certainly the precursor of the images that we find in Anger and Genet and certainly it is central to understanding what their images as well as those of later filmmakers are pointing towards. If Cocteau uses contact with the darkness as a metaphor for the artistic process, a great part of the legacy he leaves for later artists is seeing, in the homoerotic aspect of that darkness, a trope for understanding gay identity. In a very important sense, Cocteau's having created images of the queer artist and his dark lover/muse represents the beginning of a subversive process of image-making that sees that the very idea of thinking of queer desire as dark opens up a space in which people can look into the darkness and find not mere horror but power—and this power inevitably links gay identity with poetry, with imaginal creation.

Anger's *Fireworks* was one among several films he made as an emigré living in Paris. Living in Paris in the 1940s, he became something of a boy wonder in the art film world because of the provocative nature of his films. Deeply interested in magic and Satanism, Anger became a devotee of Aleistair Crowley, whose writings on the occult had a central place of importance on the formation of Anger's sensibilities. All of Anger's works, from the first films of the forties through to the last film he made in the 1960s, appeal for their inspiration to notions of magic and the power of the demonic. Continually reworking images relating to these obsessions, Anger produced films which later filmmakers—including Jean Genet—would often cite as creative influences.

Fireworks survives as a work of interest more than anything because it has so much the character of an archetypal art film made under the influence of surrealism. Hermetic and richly suggestive, the film speaks through images in a way that is both immediately compelling and confoundedly mystifying. Looking at this film, I think we are obliged to avoid asking what is this about and turn our attention instead to asking, What new way of seeing does it open up before us?

A good part of the fascination this film provides is the sheerly cinematic quality of its images. Made as a silent film and overlaid with a film score taken from music by Resphigi—the hallmark of a low-budget art film (and of a great many porno films, as well), the film looks eerie in its stark visual character—sharply lit, black-and-white, grainy 35mm images that don't at all look like anything Hollywood. What is amazing about this film is how compelling its images are given the technical simplicity with which it was executed.

The action in *Fireworks* is very simple. A young man (portrayed by Anger himself, who was seventeen at the time he made the film) awakens in his apartment, goes out into the street, looking, as Anger himself has said, for a light (for his cigarette) encounters various beefy men who display themselves in a sexually suggestive way and then dominate him in acts of violence. Returning from this waking dream, a melange of images of homoerotic attraction, the young man falls back into his bed, where he appears in a halo of light (an effect achieved by etching on the film's negative)—having gone out for a light, he returns "enlightened." Most of the film takes the form of a play between images of beefcake types showing off their bodies and harassing the character played by Anger. What makes both sets of images particularly impressive is the fact that they all seem to serve the character of the young man towards some sort of pleasure—a reversal of the usual order of things. Here the manly male is rendered as an object of fascination, a dumbly miming thing, an image of maleness itself, conjured up to serve the pleasure of a rather wistful-looking young male. The young man, slender and a bit fussy, definitely a queen, comes then to appear as the controlling source of power in the film. It's not the beefcake sailors who are calling the shots—it's the young man who desires and who goes out *intending* to be possessed. His power is magical; he lures men to him. They are unable to withstand his provocation to display muscle or violence, and thus they are the ones dominated—by his desire—in a visual equation that seems designed to disorient the viewer and to render uncertain any notion of power or masculinity.

The young man is the central figure of the film. We begin and end in his world, an apartment in which the front door is labeled "Gents" in a suggestion of toilet-sex lust. What's outside the young man's tiny corner of the world is a bigger world, labeled as a latrine, an image unequivocally suggesting a queen's search for sex among real men with the most delicate part of their manhood exposed. When he leaves his apartment, he seems indeed to be going into another dimension—and so it is. The world of the queen and the world of the real man are thus visually marked by the apartment's front door. The world outside the apartment is also shot on artificially lit sets (anticipating the later work of Fassbinder), suggesting that the public world of manliness is a stage, a highly histrionic theater where people perform for an audience—other men.

When the fey young man encounters a sailor—all the men but he are fully uniformed specimens of public manhood—he pulls the sailor into a frank display of pleasure in his own manhood. In effect, he causes the sailor to expose his own lust for manhood; even when the sailor hits the young man after this display, however, the fey boy seems to take it all in as an experience of pleasure, obliging the sailor, after the beating, to light his cigarette—a suggestion of après-sex pleasure. The images suggest homoerotic desire being bound with fire. At every point the young man encounters another man, some image of fire appears. No matter what the men around him do, no matter which way they turn, the dominant males always wind up acting at his bidding, always giving him what he wants. At the end of the little adventure, as he lies spent in his bed, we see his head garlanded with flames, recalling the imagery of Genet's novels—he is lying like a piéta, as he had earlier in a brief scene with a sailor—also anticipating Genet's and Fassbinder's *Querelle.* The fairy as the holy body, the flesh transmutated through torment—which is to say, brought to ecstasy through pain and delight. Homoerotic desire equals light equals awakening.

The effect of the film is to bracket images of archetypal maleness within images of homosexual male desire—that which is archetypically male is willed into existence through unrepentant gay lust, is proliferated by it, and returns to it in acts of holy worship—always despite itself, always unable to help itself. The idea of a real man was created by a fairy, and all real men are the love slaves of their fey benefactors. There's not a damn thing they can do about it. Perhaps most startling of all—perhaps that which continues to give the film so much impact—is how matter-of-factly all this is presented to us: of *course* it's true, of course the fairy is the magus who conjures up the image of the he-man, of

course that image is an expression of the fairy-magus's desire and consciousness.

Made just three years after *Fireworks*, *A Song of Love*, Genet's single,
completed work as director and screenwriter, stands as an important work in its
own right, even though it has never had a commercial release (most recently,
however, it is appearing in various video versions). What is most important
about this film is the way it artfully eroticizes much of what is traditionally
considered monstrous in homosexual desire—the violence, dirtiness, and
shamelessness of fascination with maleness—developing from these forms of
monstrosity a sense, finally, not of depravity but of physical and spiritual transformation.[3] Ultimately, Genet's film appears to equate monstrousness with
transgression, with violating limits of acceptability, implying in his film that all
desire is, by nature, transgressive, and that the transgressive character of the
homosexual provides a fully articulated image of desire itself.[4]

A Song of Love is a peculiar case among films. Particularly for gay filmmakers, this film is important because, like Anger's first films, it was one of the
first films to appear shortly after World War Two that helped to define a serious
basis for conversation among gay filmmakers. This conversation was shaped
from its beginning by the cinematic underground, for the underground was the
only milieu in which film work that dealt openly with lesbian and gay themes
could be allowed to develop. As a matter of historical fact, it goes without saying that in the period of the late forties and early fifties, a studio film that depicted homosexuality was unthinkable unless the whole matter was treated, à la
Franklin Pangborn and Edward Everett Horton, as a very funny but more or less
harmless joke. Hence Genet's film, barely twenty-five minutes long and shot
under makeshift conditions mostly in the Paris bar owned by the film's producer, Niko Papakatis, was important to the underground in general and to gay
filmmakers in particular because it was among the first serious art films that
dealt with homosexuality frankly and unapologetically. Through films like
Genet's, then, homosexuality depicted from the point of view of a gay filmmaker began to move from stag films to "legitimate" cinema (though at the time
A Song of Love first appeared, it was banned as pornography because of its
frank depiction of homosex—but it was accepted at least in some parts of the
art film circuit). Perhaps more important than that is the fact that, like Anger's
films (by which Genet commented, as he made *A Song of Love*, he had been
deeply impressed), Genet's single completed film seemed so fully to assume
matter-of-factly as its center the point of view of a homosexual sensibility. As
much as some queer critics like to argue over whether or not there even *is* such
a thing as a gay sensibility in art, I would argue that what one finds in Anger's
and Genet's work (and certainly in Cocteau's work) epitomizes gay sensibility
by insisting so strongly on making the desire for and fascination with maleness
so overt, so centrally present, so much a central component upon which all else
depends. Like *Fireworks*, Genet's film is imbued with such a sensibility, and
this, nearly fifty years later, in a world where it is still risky business to render

visible the sexual power of being gay, is largely what helps maintain its power, its freshness. Like Anger's *Fireworks* and Cocteau's *Blood of a Poet*, Genet's film is extraordinary in the way it presents erotic—specifically homoerotic—imagery to convey a sense of myth.

The film, in black and white and without a sound track, was shot in a bar in Paris using sets constructed to make the bar double as a prison.[5] The shooting of many of the film's exterior shots was something of a criminal act, since Genet, in choosing the Santé prison, failed to obtain permission from officials before filming.[6] The film is made up of a series of vignettes that form around certain images or pieces of action, each vignette cutting into the next in what soon becomes established as a musical pattern of elements. One such vignette depicts prisoners in adjoining cells—a younger man shot mostly in bright light and a somewhat older man shot mostly in shadows—communicating with each other between the cell walls in a display of erotic play. Paired up with the scenes cutting between the two prisoners' cells are fantasy scenes, filmed in blisteringly bright daylight in a forest, where the two prisoners are shown together, engaged in sexual games of pursuit and domination. Another recurring vignette shows a prison warder moving from cell to cell, watching the prisoners and voyeuristically enjoying their acts of sexual play and, ultimately, becoming violently involved in those games. Paired with these scenes are fantasy scenes in which the warder is nude and is with another nude man, engaged in highly stylized, romantically erotic play. Interspersed between these scenes are scenes that form a refrain to the "song" of the film: scenes shot from outside the prison in which one prisoner is shown throwing a garland of flowers to a prisoner in an adjoining cell as the latter tries to catch it. The effect of cutting between these scenes is to create a strong sense that the film is a visual song, with the variously cut vignettes forming phrases and refrains. The film, we are led to see, is a visual song of love.

The song in Genet's film consists of an assemblage of erotic and symbolic imagery that come to form a *mythos*; this *mythos* expresses the nature of desire and the character of maleness. Working clearly under the influence, by way of Anger and Cocteau, of surrealism, Genet's film is very much about using this assemblage, this mythos to lead the viewer to a point of disorientation, of *désreglement de sens*, so that when we come to the film's end, we are left not so much with a neat understanding of anything as with a disturbing sense of how violence, lust, passion, disgust, being queer and being a regular guy all fit together. In the end, this is a film that plays with the whole idea of identity—particularly male identity—in a way that will lead the careful viewer to doubt what (s)he knows about what it means to be a real man.

The strategy of the film is to present male identity in a demonic process of sexual being and becoming. This is very much a film of images—no soundtrack, lots of close-ups, very simple, often repeated action. All the images of the film concern themselves with men, more specifically with maleness; all that imagery is linked in a very formally constructed pattern that leads from a positive value to a negative value (at the beginning of the film we see a prison warder looking at men throwing a garland, and at the end we see him turning away from the same scene); and all the imagery of the film is quite literally demonic in that it is presented as instances of division, duplication and permutation. The literally demonic character of the film's imagery is then reinforced or echoed in the symbolically demonic nature of the film's imagery—the men we see are either abject criminals or a prison warder caught in the act of peeping lasciviously—and of its lines of thought—what we see comes together in a presentation of men wallowing in maleness. True to the obsessions of Genet's novels, *A Song of Love* finally takes shape as a presentation of abjection, the abjection of identity expressed as erotic desire.

Indeed, if there is one word to use in reference to this film, it is the word *demonic*. As derived from the word δαιμοαι (*daimoai*, to distribute or to divide,)[7] *demonic* denotes that type of rhetorical device through which, by means of personification, a poet (in the purest sense of the word) projects a unity as a series of divided images. This projection takes place at sites of awareness that involve crisis: for example, where the authors of the Old Testament speak of angels and devils, they are expressing the problem of human identity—the fact that good and evil are compellingly present and active as forces in human lives. Wherever this division of imagery appears, it does so as an invitation to solve a problem: how do we get the divided pieces back together into a neat unity, how do we reconcile the angels with the devils?

It should take little work to understand how common the activity of creating demonic imagery is to the imagination. Stated as I have, it would appear that the activity of demon making is one of the central and most elegant means the imagination has for working out cognitive problems. The problem that arises in this process, however, has to do with the way our culture tends to use the strong/weak alignment of paired concepts, particularly as regards concepts that relate to fundamental value (like good and bad). For Judeo-Christian culture, a problem (at least before Nietzsche) must be stated in terms of good versus evil, with evil being defined as *privation*, as the absence of good. Such a system of valuation can only point to a fundamental tendency to deny the work of the demonic in the imagination, which is always work towards awareness that moves from fragmentation to wholeness: we bring images of fragmentation into being to find a way to connect the pieces into something whole. Hence we are taught to think that the very idea of the demonic has merely to do with hell and the devil, and we have been taught to forget that the angels and the vision of heaven came into being as part of that same picture. We are taught, in effect, to sabotage the work of the demonic in the imagination by assigning some of its components a false value.

Considering what I've said about the demonic, what makes *A Song of Love* so interesting and so dangerous is the way it plays so fully with the notion of the demonic. At the most superficial level, we can see how many ways Genet uses in this film to present a strong sense of division—particularly division by twos—in his images. First of all, the film relentlessly uses cutting from one image to another, and it keeps content within a scene consistently simple so that, when we see a particular scene, we are often drawn to a single object—a face or a body, occasionally *two* bodies—deliberately set against an almost vacant backdrop. Second, the film sets up a doubled division in the action between the two main prisoners—the older man and the murderer—and between the warder and the older prisoner. Third, the cutting technique of the film involves a doubled division from "real" action to *two* species of fantasy: the scenes in which we see the prisoners and the warder in the prison, established as real time and space in the world of the film; and the scenes in which we see either the prisoners cavorting in the woods or in which we see the warder nude, writhing about the body of another nude man in highly choreographed movements set against an artificial background (the opposite, the dark double of the woods). And fourth, there is the division between the scenes of the film that show men relating to each other as whole bodies: scenes in which we can take the action as having a literal meaning, and scenes in which men relate to each other as arms hanging out a window passing a garland—scenes which impress themselves upon us as being immediately symbolic, as suggesting not only something about the two prisoners but about men in general.

Given the character of Genet's work on paper, it should be clear that his division of characters into many prisoners and one prison warder is an expression of contempt for the notion of dividing value into good and evil. In *A Song of Love*, good and evil are replaced by a keeper and a group of convicts—and *everyone* is in a prison. In this prison division is presented visually as a site for communication: the prisoners tap on the walls between their cells or share a cigarette through a hole in the wall, and the warder looks furtively through peepholes as they communicate with him by playing with their bodies and toying with him. The warder is the only character in the film who can literally move freely from cell to cell—but this freedom only leads to his disintegration. Appearing first as a simple image of the law, the warder is quickly revealed to be a sort of criminal—a peeping tom who is alarmed, is brought to shame, when he is made to reflect upon himself (he is divided within himself) after he is caught watching a prisoner stroke his dick. Ironically, communication between prisoners is presented as being more authentic, more honest and open than that between warder and prisoner. While the prisoners are presented as being literally contained but spiritually open and self-aware, the warder, as representative of the law, and by extension, of the logos, the received order of the dominant culture, is presented matter-of-factly as being sneaky and self-deceiving.

What is communicated at all these sites? Relentlessly, what is communicated is the nature of identity rendered as icons linked in a three-part formulation: identity equals the desire for maleness equals abjection. A man is either a convict locked in a chain of lust and violence with another convict or he is a prison warder caught looking through a peephole while playing with himself. The consciousness-killing system of splitting between positive value and the absence of value is replaced by a system of calmly conscious, continually doubled value. As images of maleness are presented, they aren't offered as an opposition of queer/straight, outcast/good citizen; they are offered in a linking of legitimate with criminal. What is ordinarily given as abnormal is here given as simply, pervasively true.

What strikes me about the system of values that Genet constructs with this film is its refusal to allow a comfortable distinction between positive and negative, between good and bad. The warder is implicated in the crimes of the convicts; he is presented as being every bit as depraved as they are in the pursuit of lust. What separates them from him, at least for awhile, is his lack of consciousness. The prisoners are almost pure consciousness in this film. Aware of their bodies and their desires at every point we see them, they seem unable to resist or to hide an awareness of their nature. That nature is desire, desire for another: for the older prisoner, the desire is for possession of the younger man, for the younger man, the desire is for maintaining the game of seduction. Their bodies are almost always in motion, motion that speaks without sound, motion that almost at every point expresses longing for or longing within maleness. The warder, given his social position, dryly envisioned in the film as a uniform, is, in effect, hiding from the other men, unconsciously enjoying them, unaware that he too is engaged in a dance of desire until the mechanism of his unconsciousness—his looking furtively—is made to turn on him as he is found out. Hiding takes place in the open space of the prison, consciousness is contained within cells, but cannot be held there. It escapes through the fluid medium of imagination, the very engine that drives desire.

In *A Song of Love* all desire seems to intersect at the image of the younger prisoner—the warder and the older prisoner focus their imagination on him. In the younger prisoner's image is focused much of the film's presentation of desire—his image is, for the world of the film, the most comprehensive depiction of desire. Thus invested with meaning, the younger prisoner functions as an image in which the demonic fragmentation of desire is reconciled into an image that is angel and devil at the same time. In Genet's system of thought, this makes it necessary to show him as both the supremely desired and most abjectly fallen creature in the film. The younger prisoner is, in fact, a murderer, as we learn from the inscription *meurtrier* above his cell door. Murderers appear prominently in Genet's novels, particularly *Miracle of the Rose* and *Querelle de Brest*. In *Querelle*, for instance, Genet describes the character Querelle, who is a murderer, as having (like the film's younger prisoner) a splendidly mystical, hypermasculine sort of beauty:

> Querelle was not used to the idea, one that had never really been formulated, that he was a monster. He considered, he observed his past with an ironic smile, frightened and tender at the same time, to the extent that this past became confused with what he himself was. Thus might a young boy whose soul is evident in his eyes, but who has been metamor-

phosed into an alligator, even if he were not fully conscious of his hor-
rendous head and jaws, consider his scaly body, his solemn, gigantic tail,
with which he strikes the water or the beach or brushes against that of
other monsters, and which extends him with the same touching, heart-
rending and indestructible majesty as the train of a robe, adorned with
lace, with crests, with battles, with a thousand crimes, worn by a Child
Empress, extends her.[8]

This description exemplifies the way that Genet, in his novels, posits a connection between crime, the physicality of masculinity, and the transgressive nature
of beauty. In Genet's formulation, crime becomes recorded in man's body as
form, which is to say that crime shapes the body. The body thus shaped becomes a representation, an image of action. As representation, this image yields
formality of construction as being central to its being, and in this formality
consists its beauty. What is represented in this image is the character of crime;
here, specifically, what is represented is the character of the supreme crime:
cold-blooded murder. The scope of the crime thus describes the scope of the
image the body records: it is an image of humanity monstrously enlarged to a
potential for meaning through transgression, which is to say, rendered supremely meaningful through transgression. As a well-established theme in
Genet's novels, then, the beauty of criminal, hypermasculine men appears in
Genet's film, as Richard Dyer has noted, as a classical foregrounding of form.[9] I
think that what Genet is asserting with this powerfully invested form is that
what is most true about men and maleness is to be seen most clearly in what is
conceived as being the most abject of male types. Abjection means literally that
which is cast off, that which is rejected. Genet seems to be inviting us, in the
form of the murderer, to consider what is true about being a man by asking us to
look—through the eyes of two other men—at this supreme cast-off: a nasty
little punk who kills people. And the point here is not, I think, to understand
such an image. It is an irrational image. The point is to treat it like a holy icon,
an image meant to spur deep contemplation, an image meant to lead to self-
awareness and transformation.

　　While I do think that the younger prisoner plays an extraordinary function
as an image of desire, I would stop short of saying that the film is "about" him.
The first several times I saw the film, I was seduced into thinking that it was
mostly about the two prisoners—the murderer and the older man who have
adjoining cells (and fantasy lives). After looking at the film again, I've decided
that the film is as much about the guard as it is about anything else. The guard is
established, from the beginning of the film, as the eye through which the film
looks. It is his figure that first appears; it is he who sees the garland being
passed from one hand to another. It is he who sees the prisoners, and in the way
he sees them, I am obliged to ask myself now whether what he sees is an expression as much of his own desire as it is of the desire between prisoners. The
guard, by definition, is in control here. He alone can move from cell to cell; he

alone can actually go in and see each prisoner. His uniform and his gun are emblems of his social position; and yet so much of the film has to do with his being undone, even as he remains in his position of power. He is caught looking through peepholes, and it is clear that the prisoners enjoy the fact that he is watching. His awareness that he has been found out fills him with rage and, having been thus dominated by the prisoners who catch him, especially (appropriately enough) the young murderer, he seeks to dominate another prisoner, but his attempt at domination quickly turns into a sexual game—whipping and playing with guns—and he is found out again. As we see the two principal prisoners in fantasy scenes, we also see the warder in similar scenes, as if to suggest that all the fantasies we see are really his. He is in control of this world, he shapes it, and yet it continues to turn on him.

How does it turn on him? By forcing him into consciousness, a consciousness of his own nature—and that means the nature of his sexual character. As long as he thinks he isn't being observed, he moves from cell to cell, watching the men play with their dicks as he strokes his own through his trousers—lost for awhile in unconscious pleasure. When he is forced into awareness of the nature of his pleasure, he is mortified, shamed, and yet he is unable, even after having been brought into this consciousness, to escape from it. He leaves the prison defeated as a real man—he has been found out—and yet this is not the last image of the film. The last image of the film is that of the garland being caught, an image of sexual fulfillment between men. This is as much the guard's image, as much his fantasy, as it is that of the prisoners. The fact that he is walking away from it at the end of the film doesn't matter, which makes Genet's including it that much more hilarious. By then the film has so clearly established him as the film's consciousness that it seems ineluctable that he is the one for whom the garland has been caught. Identity equals desire equals betrayal equals abjection. Abjection is the truth of maleness—the truth of being a man is what men reject about themselves. The truth of being a man is all there in the image of a sociopathic, cock-hungry punk.

All men are brothers in the dark of this artfully vicious little film. The film uses chains—chains of flowers, chains of men, chains of imprisonment—to establish a continuity between the characters of all men. This is *all* men's sexual nature we are seeing. We are seeing a catalogue of the forms of relationship between men: play, domination, lust, disgust, possession—all of them leading into one another, all of them amounting to the same thing, perhaps. But not quite—the prisoners are, ironically, free in their abjection, because it allows them to live freely within a consciousness of their own nature. The guard fights against his own abjection, unable to wrest himself from it, unwilling, it seems, to give in to consciousness of it. Hence he is left with shame, and the prisoners are left with ecstasy. The law undoes itself and the lawless reign—but only by virtue of having been named lawless.

In this film the demonic division permits a sense of the angelic only at the site where all men join together in their nature—and that point is the point of abjection. The truth of male identity is that it is a process of desire, identity is desiring-for, and that desiring-for is finally a movement towards consciousness. Consciousness here is the pleasure/pain of recognition, enjoyed by the outcast, the criminal, as reveling in violence, felt as humiliation, as deflation, by the warder whose medium is unconsciousness. The faggot, aware of his identity as man, is aware that that identity is desiring-for-maleness; the guard, given as certified man, is first unaware of his desiring-for-maleness, because it has been handed to him in a form that is self-proclaimed, a form that does not permit questions. When brought to consciousness of his desiring-for-maleness, the guard is revealed to be a false man, he is found out as a fairy, he is canceled out. The prison is there to contain the truth that maleness means desiring-for-maleness; the men who live in awareness of this truth must be contained, while outside the prison the truth must be hidden under a uniform. The convict's delight is the guard's shame; the song of love is a treatise on abjection, and this treatise is, after all, a meditation on beauty.

Looking back on these three films seen as a set of films related both historically and aesthetically to each other, a number of points of interest present themselves. It is remarkable how fully Cocteau's, Anger's and Genet's films appear to play with Hollywood traditions that relate to the depiction of gay people. Both *Fireworks* and *A Song of Love* are suffused with the presence of film noir, both literally bathed in the presence of light and dark, both obsessed with the particular fantasy of maleness that relates to city streets, nighttime, the threat (or perhaps the promise?) of crime and the view of the world seen through the eyes of the criminal. Anger's criminal is the fey, young, citified queen, decadent and wholly given over to his own appetite for lust. Genet's criminals are all the people on the landscape he paints; convicts and keeper are all criminals, luxuriating in the darkness of their own excesses, illuminated by the power of their intense desire. The people these two films show us are the gunsels of the forties film noir, transformed from comically reduced support players (like Peter Lorre and Elisha Cook) to sublimely enlarged central figures. As small as these films are—each is less than half and hour long and was made on the thinnest of budgets—they display a remarkable artistry at showing something that is the antithesis of what had existed around them.

What had existed around them was a limited number of images of gay people rendered as simple human failures—insignificant characters bound for doom. What we see in the films of Cocteau, Anger and Genet are images of the transgressive homosexual—the mad artist and the remorseless punk—made to appear as monumental, as an image of raw visual power to speak back to the dominant order of things. What makes these films succeed in speaking is, I think, largely a matter of how simply they present the matter-of-factness of homosexual desire. Just as the world around Cocteau, Anger and Genet could not bear to speak openly about homosexuality, the three artists themselves made films that started out not from a point of defending the legitimacy of homosexuality but rather of simply presenting *as given* the power of homosexual desire. Offering little explication, little in the way of asking us to understand or sympathize with the characters the films presents, both films throw us into a world of homosexual desire *in medias res*, a world in which everything arises out of and expresses that desire so ineluctably that we—all audiences, really, but most especially gay ones—are obliged through looking at them to do two things. First we are obliged to see that the invisibility of homosexuality can be undone; indeed, that it can be replaced with another way of seeing that allows us to see how very present homosexuality is: it is not an insignificant thing, it is a powerful thing. Second, we are obliged to see that the world constructed as an order of heterosexual desire is not a necessary vision at all; on the contrary, it is possible to envision a world in which heterosexuality doesn't even exist, and that world can be seen as full of power.

Genet's influence as a literary and cinematic presence has been remarkable.[10] To my way of thinking, what makes his work so important is the way he so seamlessly builds an image of the world in which all that polite society says about itself is erased and is replaced with so much of what is denied or rejected. In Genet's work, the image of the world is an image of people, an image formed by all the human characteristics that we don't ordinarily like to look at: all men are butt-fucking goons, soulless killers or abject pansies; in this world, women barely exist—where they appear, they are strangers, always at the edge of things. The world thus conceived is a world of horror—utter horror transformed through the act of looking. Genet's world asks for nothing so much as to be looked at as a vision, as an act of pure seeing—artifice mounted upon artifice in a way that clears away all the crap in what people tell themselves about who and what they are. This image-world would simply be a monumental creation of vice if it were not for its formality. It is so clearly a construction that it cannot help but be seen as an invitation to see through what is being presented. To see Genet's monsters is really to see through them—to see that what we say about being a man is really a pack of lies, a superstructure of chaotic lies made to look like order. The apparent order of the prison is really just a mess that looks imposing, like a uniform or a gun. The whole purpose of the prison is to contain the truth, which is that the real difference between the lawlessness of the criminal and the lawlessness hidden *under* a uniform is that the criminal is aware of himself. Sex between men is not, as William Burroughs has said, about love; it's about recognition.

Because he succeeded at producing only one complete film, Genet has functioned as a precursor to other gay filmmakers primarily through the force of his style and his thematic preoccupations as a writer. As we will see in the discussion that follows, for instance, Genet's influence on one such filmmaker, Rainer Werner Fassbinder, arises, if we are to believe the testimony that Fassbinder has left behind, solely from the latter's long-standing obsession with and admiration for Genet's last novel, *Querelle de Brest*. In his cinematic treatment of Genet's novel, Fassbinder creates an extraordinarily complex film that treats the notion of monstrous homosexuality in a way that both echoes and extrapolates from what Genet's work presents.

NOTES

1. For information concerning Cocteau's development as a filmmaker, I am deeply in debt to Francis Steegmuller's incomparable biography of Cocteau. See Steegmuller, *Cocteau: A Biography* (Boston: Little, Brown and Company, 1970), 363.

2. Arthur Evans, *Jean Cocteau and His Films of Orphic Identity* (Philadelphia: Arts Alliance Press, 1977), 35.

3. Writing about Genet's film, but also about the mystique that has been constructed around 'Genet' the cultural icon, Richard Dyer notes: "'Genet' is central to the construction of a major strain of gay culture. He is both a known set of symbols for a homosexual existence and a reference point for argument about what homosexual existence is or should be." See Dyer, *Now you see it: Studies on lesbian and gay film* (London and New York: Routledge, 1990), 48.

4. In arriving at this reading of Genet, I have drawn considerably from the discussion of Lacan's theory of desire that Jonathan Dollimore develops in *Sexual Dissidence: Augustine to Wilde, Freud to Foucault* (Oxford: Clarendon Press, 1992), 201-2.

5. Jane Giles writes that *A Song of Love* was shot between April and June 1950 in the forest of Milly, south of Paris, where Genet's friend and protector Jean Cocteau lived, and on sets built in *La Rose Rouge*, a Paris nightclub owned by Nico Papakatis, who financed the film. See Giles, "Un chant d'amour," *Artforum*, January 1988: 102.

6. In her book on Genet's film, Jane Giles notes that the "exterior stone wall seen at the very beginning and end of the film belonged to Genet's former prison, La Santé, where he wrote the predominantly biographical novel, *Miracle de la rose*, and was filmed without the necessary permission of the authorities." See Giles, *The Cinema of Jean Genet: Un chant d'amour* (London: British Film Institute, 1991), 18.

7. Angus Fletcher, *Allegory: The Theory of a Symbolic Mode* (Ithaca: Cornell University Press), 1990, 42.

8. Jean Genet, *Querelle*, trans. Anselm Hollo (New York: Grove Weidenfeld, 1974), 14.

9. Dyer, *Now you see it*, 55.

10. For an excellent discussion of Genet's cinematic legacy, see Richard Dyer, "Chapter Two: Shades of Genet," in Dyer, *Now You See It: Studies in Lesbian and Gay Film* (New York and London: Routledge, 1990), 47-101.

CHAPTER 4

Son of Genet: Fassbinder's *Querelle*

Rainer Werner Fassbinder was widely regarded, among friends and enemies alike, as being a monstrous character. Fassbinder was well-known for his excesses: he ate excessively, drank alcohol and took drugs excessively, and overworked himself and his film crews to exhaustion. His personal relationships with coworkers and lovers also bore the mark of monstrous excess. Working closely with a small group of technicians and actors, Fassbinder built a number of professional relationships by the great force of his creative energy, only to destroy many of those relationships by the force of his emotional volatility. His lover relationships, mostly with other men, tended to be intense, often publicly histrionic affairs; two them ended with his estranged lover's committing suicide. In every aspect of his life, a life so completely and intensely lived in public, this remarkable man exemplifies to a monumental degree the contrary forces involved in creativity.

In 1982 Rainer Fassbinder died in his sleep from a drug overdose, leaving behind one of the most remarkable creative legacies in film history. His last film, an adaptation of Genet's *Querelle de Brest*, was released just a few weeks before he died. The film earned Fassbinder both critical acclaim and condemnation: in the first few weeks of the film's release, it won a prize at the Venice Film Festival and was harshly condemned by the Vatican. After his death in June 1982, critics began to speak of Fassbinder's last film as his "testament," as if, assuming he had committed suicide, he had left his film *Querelle* as a recapitulation of his entire life's work. The case for looking at *Querelle* as a sort of testament has considerable merit.[1] Like Fassbinder's many other films, *Querelle* seems clearly focused on presenting the process by which people victimize each other in everyday relationships. More specifically, *Querelle* appears to relate with other of the director's films that treat homosexual characters as being social monsters—either as criminal characters who relentlessly, fiendishly exploit the people close to them (as in *Fox and His Friends*, released in 1975, or *The Marriage of Maria Braun*, released in 1979) or as hopelessly powerless misfits who live at the mercy of the world around them (as in *A Year of Thirteen Moons*, released in 1980). In *Querelle*, the themes of criminality and victimization in personal relationships take a powerful and disturbing form: a form through which the monstrousness of homosexual relationships is posited as being emblematic of sexual relationships in general.

Querelle is a complex film rigorously organized around four themes: human relationships as sexual games; the dynamics of game-playing as being founded on the creation of and play among identities expressed as images; image-production as a process whereby meaning is destroyed; and the process of the destruction of meaning as a process involving acts of betrayal and collusion. As these themes are presented as elements of the film's fictional narrative, they are also echoed in the film's principal structural devices. These devices include the character of the film's *mise en scène*, which emphasizes a sense of artificiality in the world of the film; structuring certain scenes either as doubles or as inversions of other scenes; and structuring certain scenes as fragments, as elements of the narrative that are not brought to a logical conclusion.

All that happens in *Querelle* seems to depend on what the character Querelle does or how other people react to him. A sailor just arrived in the city of Brest, Querelle (portrayed by Brad Davis) is a handsome murderer, thief and smuggler who intends to use an accomplice, a sailor from his ship named Vic (portrayed by Dieter Schidor, the film's producer), to move a shipment of heroin undetected past customs officials and into the city. The ship's captain, Lt. Seblon (portrayed by Franco Nero) is sexually obsessed with Querelle, who knows this and who, in return, feels contempt for him. Querelle responds to the lieutenant's desire by subtly taunting him.

Once ashore, Querelle finds his brother Robert (portrayed by Harry Baur in an uncredited role), who is the lover of Mme Lysiane (Jeanne Moreau). Together with her husband Nono (Günther Kauffman), Mme Lysiane runs the brothel La Feria,[2] where sailors, criminals and even the police come together in a common social meeting ground. Querelle meets Nono through Robert and arranges for his shipment of heroin to be sold to a customer.

Returning to the ship, Querelle enlists Vic's help to get the heroin off the ship; after this is accomplished, Querelle murders Vic. To atone for this murder, Querelle engages in one of the Feria's well-known rituals: he plays dice with Nono, the stakes of the game being that if Querelle wins, Querelle gets to have sex with Mme Lysiane; if he loses, he must submit himself to being sodomized by Nono. Deliberately losing, Querelle becomes Nono's catamite. When Nono brags of his triumph to Robert, Querelle and Robert fight. Subsequently, as the rumor spreads of Nono's sodomizing Querelle, the policeman Mario approaches Querelle and sodomizes him.

Meanwhile, the stonemason Gil (portrayed by the actor who portrays Robert) murders another stonemason, Theo, after the latter taunts him sexually, implying he is a passive sodomite. With the help of his girlfriend's brother, Roger (Laurent Malet), with whom he has a homoerotic attraction, Gil flees the police and finds a hiding place in an abandoned prison. Querelle finds Gil with the help of Roger, goes to him and offers to help him escape the city.

To accomplish this, Querelle devises a robbery plan and a disguise to make Gil look identical to Robert. Donning the disguise, Gil sneaks into the city and ambushes Lt. Seblon, seeking to steal the latter's money. Seblon resists, Gil shoots him, wounding him lightly, but still managing to escape with the lieutenant's money.

Returning to his hideout, Gil meets Querelle, and the two men confess their love for each other. Gil sets out to leave Brest and Querelle goes to Nono, betraying Gil by passing on information about his escape plans. Nono passes this information on to the police through Mario; Gil is caught, confesses to the murders of Theo and Vic (the latter confession being, of course, a lie), and denies having robbed the lieutenant. Now stripped of his disguise, Gil is brought before Lt. Seblon, who surprises the police by affirming that Gil is not the man who robbed him.

While Gil's escape and capture have unfolded, Querelle has abandoned Nono and Mario and has become Mme Lysiane's lover, leaving Robert in a state of humiliation. Seblon, finding Querelle listening to his tape-recorded diary (in which Seblon reveals his obsession for the sailor) confronts Querelle, revealing he knows who actually killed Vic. Querelle goes to Mme Lysiane in a drunken stupor, confesses to being a "fairy," and leaves with Lt. Seblon, begging to be taken as the latter's lover. As the film ends, Mme Lysiane and Robert reunite as lovers after Lysiane reads Robert's life in the tarot cards, learning from them that Robert does not have a brother.

The principal theme the film presents is the notion that personal relationships are sexual games. These games involve people, almost exclusively men, playing with values defined in terms of elements of male sexuality, so that the games all seem to be aimed at affirming what it means essentially to be a real man. In the way the film presents these games, however, what emerges finally is that what it means to be a real man is indecipherable: "real man" means *nothing*.

The emptiness of the meaning of manly games is established in one of the early scenes of the film, that in which Mme Lysiane dances with her lover Robert while her husband plays dice at the Feria's bar. As Lysiane and Robert dance, the camera cuts to Nono. He is playing dice with Mario the policeman (portrayed by Burckhard Driest), pictured here in fetishistic leatherman attire. Nono and Mario, it soon develops, form one of the many pairs of doubles that appear in the film. Nono the brothelkeeper almost always appears in the film together with Mario the corrupt policeman. Just as Nono serves the police as an informant, Mario serves Nono as an accomplice in the latter's underworld dealings (for example, the drug deal which Querelle arranges with Nono). Both men are physical embodiments of masculine stereotypes: both men are rough-looking, physically imposing, and self-confident—alternate versions of each other, this alterity accentuated by the fact that Mario is white and Nono is black. Given the way these two characters are identified so early as a pair who embody images of stereotypical maleness, Steven Shaviro notes:

> [Nono and Mario] exude supreme masculine authority as a result of having subjected their wills to a harsh, impersonal discipline. They attain perfect manhood by negating their own desires and identifying instead with an ideal, transcendent phallic order. Nono enjoys fucking Querelle and other males (except for Robert, who alone remains inaccessible to him, and who—despite his denials—he therefore still desires), but claims, "I never understood how anybody could fall in love with a man." He maintains control by indulging in a pleasure with "absolutely no emotion" attached; his credo—stated as he directly faces the camera and repeated in a title card—is "They knew why the were risking nothing, that nothing was muddying the purity of their games. No passion." As for Mario, he even more perfectly embodies phallic authority and pres-tige. Mario conflates the glamour of the outlaw with the authority of the cop; he exists at the ironic point where (homosexual) transgression be-comes complicit with dominant (heterosexual) power.[3]

Thus introduced into the film, Nono and Mario stand in the scene as background reflections of the image that Robert's presence in the scene creates, namely that of a man acting out his identity in terms of a sexual ritual or game (the dance with Lysiane).

Interrupting this game just as he is playing a game of his own (the dice game which, we soon learn, is also a sexually charged ritual), Nono shouts to Robert that the bar is closed, and Lysiane responds that Robert is staying with her for the night. Mario questions Nono about his wife's rejoinder: is Nono not jealous at the thought of his wife being with another man? After all, says Mario, to be jealous would be normal. Nono coolly responds, "What is normal?" and takes a drink, returning Mario's smirk with a cold stare. Nono's question, the question posed by a man who knows his wife is being unfaithful to him, thus obliges us to de-center the naturalness of the desire evident between Lysiane and Robert on two levels: first, Nono's reaction clearly identifies what we now recognize as the openly adulterous attraction between Lysiane and Robert; and second, Nono's admission that, in their marriage, transgression is part of the marriage bargain itself decriminalizes the act of adultery—here, being unfaithful is part of being true—and thus erases the difference between *Vergehen* and *Treue*, or between perversity (in the sense of erring from the right path) and fidelity (in the sense of keeping on the right path).[4]

The entire exchange between Lysiane, Mario and Nono is played to emphasize how much a question of ritual play the whole matter of relationships is. In this scene, establishing who has the power in a relationship, defining the boundaries of proper behavior seem to be activities that play themselves out not so much through individual people as through individual roles behind which no strongly discernible individuals exist. Given the way the actors deliver their lines—speaking in a dull, affectless monotone, giving the impression they are sleepwalking—we are, as viewers, denied the pleasure of losing ourselves in our own emotional reactions to the action we see before us, because the flatness of the character portrayals makes it unlikely that we will either identify with this or that character. This fact obliges us to retain a critical awareness of the roles we see being played before us in the scene. This awareness allows the action and imagery of the scene to suggest that assuming a (particularly male) identity is a matter of role-playing and image-production.

Another scene in the film focuses on sexual game-playing among men so as to show the emptiness of the game. This is the scene in which Querelle, having killed Vic, goes to Nono and agrees to play dice, ostensibly to win Lysiane's sexual favors. Hearing Querelle profess without any trace of passion that he desires Lysiane greatly, Nono toys with Querelle as the two men discuss the rules of the game: if Nono wins, he earns the privilege of sodomizing Querelle; and if Querelle wins, he wins the right to have sex with Mme Lysiane. It is transparent to Nono that Querelle is not the least bit interested in winning, which fact reveals that, in playing the game of dice, Querelle is also playing a psychological game with Nono. By playing with Nono in this way, Querelle both affirms his position of power with respect to Nono—he affirms his willingness to fight, man to man, to enjoy sexual favors with a woman, thereby affirming his active sexuality—and makes it completely clear that he really wants to surrender his position of power by submitting to the possibility that he might lose the game of dice. Usually, we would guess, the men who play dice with Nono actually want to have sex with their favorite woman, agreeing to play with Nono because they actually desire women badly enough to run the risk of being unmanned. The dynamics of the dice game under such conditions places Nono in the position of control that determines whether men are allowed to act out their maleness positively.

By approaching the game as he has, Querelle has upset the power dynamics in a way that appears both unique and intriguing to Nono. If Nono were to win fairly, he would retain and use the power to subjugate another man by sodomizing him. Querelle, however, fully intends to lose the game, which indeed he does, by cheating. By rigging the game, Querelle accomplishes two things: first, he foregrounds the emptiness of the game's power play; second, he reverses the power positions of active and passive partner in the transaction, revealing that, in this instance at least, control, and hence power, reside with the loser rather than the winner. By manipulating the game as he does, Querelle exposes the emptiness of an element of archetypal male identity; namely, the idea that the aggressor, the one "on top," is the real man, the person with real power. By cheating, by betraying the game, Querelle upsets the distribution of power and thus disturbs Mario's (and the viewer's) sense of clarity about *who, between the aggressor and the passive partner, the real man is.*

Once he has lost, Querelle denies his willingness to submit by warning Nono "not to try any funny business," by which he means that Nono is not to try to overpower him with too vigorous a performance or with an unmanly show of affection. Querelle, preparing to submit willingly to anal sex, tells his partner that he is "no fairy" and that he is only giving his "ass." In keeping with the film's inveterate strategy of presenting tacit admissions of homosexual desire side by side with assertions of heterosexual maleness, Querelle approaches the reality of the deflowering he has transparently, willingly sought out with vehement assertions that he is "on top of things" in the matter. As Nono—portrayed, we must remember, by a large, imposing, muscular black man—laughs at Querelle's warnings, Querelle and he fight briefly, and Querelle easily knocks him down, a victory that looks unconvincing, given the size advantage that Nono has over Querelle's much smaller, wiry form.

Having thus gained the physical advantage over his opponent, Querelle, whom we have already seen murder a man, deigns inexplicably to refrain from knocking Nono unconscious. Pausing to allow Nono to arise from the bed on which he has fallen, Querelle stands face to face with his opponent, who assumes the sailor's formal standing rest position, arms locked behind his back. Recognizing in this gesture a common male bond with Nono, Querelle engages in a bit of man talk with him, asking about his history in the service. Hearing the brief details of Nono's past in their common fraternal order, Querelle resumes his preparations, without further ado, for Nono's sodomizing him. The effect of this exchange is to assert that once the two men have established to each other that they are real men, there is no problem with their having sex with each other: only real men are permitted to break the rules of manhood. This agreement among Nono and Querelle thus places sexual transgression at the center of sexual normalcy.

At this point, the scene cuts quickly to create a wide shot of the room, showing Nono and Querelle from a greater distance. In what appears to be a bit of diabolical humor, as Querelle drops his trousers, lies down and allows Nono to penetrate him, the camera shows the figures of the two men in the left half of the frame, while the entire right half of the frame is taken up by the image of a large bird in a cage: a big white cockatoo. Effectively splitting the screen into two images that mirror each other with lewd humor, this shot presents a multivalent deflowering of maleness: we see, from a distance, the rather comically diminished forms of two men with their buttocks not fully bared but draped in unattractive boxer shorts, emptying the shot of any erotic content; and nearer to us, we see the punning image of the large caged cock, comically bobbing, displaying its crest in an involuntary gesture of courtship, and idiotically blinking its eyes straight into the camera. The shot, depicting Querelle's ritual "execution," his loss of manhood, appears artfully constructed to diminish the meaning of that loss. This diminution is accomplished by removing erotic content from the image, by moving that image out of what, in standard film iconography, is the principal position of interest on the screen (by reducing the size of the images of the men and by moving the figures of the men from center screen to screen left) and by placing, in screen right position, a shot filmed in close-up, which is to say (monstrously) enlarged. What this monstrous enlargement shows is an image of a visual dirty joke.

Further undermining the meaning of Querelle's loss of his manhood occurs in the shots that follow. As Nono begins to thrust into Querelle's rectum, we see a close-up of Nono's face, filmed through a filter that adds a hazy, soft, dreamy quality to his face. Clearly exhibiting pleasure as he has intercourse with Querelle, Nono looks into the camera and says, "Now this is how I like you." It appears here that Nono is addressing the audience as much as Querelle, suggesting that what is true for Nono and Querelle is true for the rest of us as well. This would imply that the film intends here not to give the viewer pleasure directly, but rather to filter that pleasure through an act of *Publikumsbeschimpfung* through which the audience, like Querelle in the scene before us, is humiliated and betrayed. In fact, by pausing the film briefly to address the audience through Nono, Fassbinder essentially reveals himself as a presence in the film—a monstrous, criminal voice speaking through Nono—to implicate the audience in the perverse dynamics that underlie the scene. By perverse dynamics, I mean the process whereby Fassbinder has seduced the viewer into looking with fascination, with pleasure, at the crimes presented in the film: murder, betrayal, and deviant sex. This places the film's strategy close to that of Genet who, as Jeffrey Malkan observes, identifying the artist (Genet himself) with the criminal, betrays the audience by exposing their fascination with crime as a form of transgressive pleasure that implicates them in crime itself.[5]

The next shot shows Querelle, at first wincing in pain, then declaring that the new feeling of a penis inside him is "not that bad." Humiliation brings a surprise: pleasure. As Nono continues thrusting, he passionately strokes the contours of Querelle's body, shot in close-up; contradicting his earlier warning that Nono is not to show anything resembling affection, Querelle permits Nono to continue caressing him. Thus Querelle betrays himself by freely allowing Nono to violate him doubly: by allowing himself to be sodomized and by allowing Nono to caress him passionately. As Nono prepares to ejaculate, he begins thrusting vigorously, at which point the camera, betraying the audience further by denying the viewer the pornographic pleasure of seeing the two men come to a conclusion, cuts to the following scene. Thus the scene finally betrays the viewer by denying us the pleasure of seeing Querelle's "execution" brought to its conclusion. As the conclusion *is* the execution, the scene has effectively deconstructed itself entirely.

The scene next returns to the ship: Lt. Seblon has summoned Querelle to commend him for volunteering for extra duty. Querelle, blackened with coal dust, appears from below deck to answer the lieutenant's summons. Covered with dust, he is now a blackface version of Nono. This image of Querelle adds yet another, doubly darkly humorous diminution to the ritual of his execution: having been sodomized by a big black man, having taken an erect penis in his rectum, Querelle now appears before us, wearing the image of the violator's body upon his own. Answering the lieutenant's commendation of his industriousness, Querelle answers rather sweetly that he took the extra duty "down below" to "help out a buddy," looking in the direction of the shore and the Feria with a wistful smile as he speaks. As he appears before us, Querelle implies that he has sealed a bond of male friendship with Nono; indeed, that he has taken Nono into (and now onto) himself by allowing himself to assume the image of a black man as a favor to "his buddy." This places Querelle's act of submission within the framework of affirmative male bonding, while admitting at the same time that the specific nature of that bond involves a masochistic undoing of maleness. Hence, in the logic of the film, being a man and being unmanned amount to the same thing.

Later in the film, we find another scene that deconstructs the sexual games men play. This one shows Robert and Querelle fighting after Robert has learned that Querelle has allowed himself to be used as a sexual object by Nono. As the brothers fight, the camera cuts between shots of Querelle and Robert fighting and shots of a young man, a near double of Querelle, reenacting the Stations of the Cross, thus linking Querelle's humiliating confrontation with his brother to the humiliation of Christ carrying the Cross to His own Crucifixion. As these shots cut back and forth, the narrator comments: "The two brothers resembled each other more and more. The combat in which they engaged was more like a lovers' quarrel." The process of doubling in this scene effects an almost dizzying deterritorialization and signification of meaning. Robert and Querelle, referred to in the film as virtual doubles of each other, struggle before us as representatives of opposite positions in a male hierarchy: Robert, on the one side, is the outraged *normal* male, while Querelle, on the other side, is the defensive, transgressive sodomite. Querelle, the willing subject of venal passion, is further doubled in the image of Christ's Passion, presented as a reenactment, that is, as a double.

The multivalent doubling that occurs in this scene has the effect of divesting the conflict between Querelle and Robert of any content. All the images of that conflict that we see are presented as canceling each other out: Robert's identity as a man is canceled by Querelle's failure to maintain the image of macho man, a failure he has effected with Nono's help; Querelle's identity in the film as a murderer and as a suspected fairy is bracketed by his identification in the scene not with Christ, but rather with a simulated image of Christ; and finally, Robert's assertion that he is punishing his brother for the latter's willing surrender of his masculinity is nullified by the narrator's assertion that the two men are fighting like lovers, like men who have already surrendered their manhood. Significantly, the fight scene ends without either brother winning full advantage over the other: neither man can dominate the other; they can only cancel each other out. As an alarm sounds, an alarm that could be a police siren or a boxing ring bell, Querelle and Robert simply stop fighting and go on about their business. This end to the fight gives the entire event the quality of a ritual exercise or game governed by rules whose arbitrariness emphasizes how meaningless the game finally is. Why, after all, would two enraged men suddenly stop a knife fight just because they hear an alarm sounding? The alarm could be read as a sound signaling the end of a work shift or a sports competition: work is done, the round is over, those are the rules, and that simply is the way things are.

At still other points in the film, we get a sense of the emptiness of games through the actions of two other characters: Lt. Seblon and Mme Lysiane. For instance, late in the film we see Lt. Seblon talking with police, who have come on board his ship to try to get information about the murders of Vic and Theo. As viewers we suspect, at this point, that Seblon knows clearly that Querelle is connected with these crimes. Thus the viewer is placed into a position of collusion with Seblon as he toys with the police who, interestingly enough, believe that the murders have something to do with jealous rivalries among violent homosexual men on board the ship and in the city. Using his position of authority as a shield, Seblon denies to the police, with obvious bemusement, that he is in a position to know anything either about the murders or about any other dealings by such "shady characters" as the police describe. Again, as viewers, we know already that the Lieutenant himself *is* one of these shady characters: he lusts after his own men and he looks for sex in public latrines. A representative of the male order of things—he is a ship's officer—Seblon uses his position to betray that order, and by so doing, he protects and nurtures the monstrous order of criminality and sexual transgression.

As regards Mme Lysiane's place in the network of games among men, it is interesting to note that she is the only female character in the film (the whores of the Feria, who appear as nonspeaking background figures, are all portrayed by male actors *en travestie*). As a woman, Mme Lysiane lives at the periphery of men's games, maintaining her position as a player only to the extent that she helps men to play for power with other men. Part of Lysiane's attraction for Robert derives from her status as a trophy: Robert uses her to affirm his own manhood by claiming her from her own husband. Lysiane realizes, from the beginning, that Robert truly loves only Querelle, and that nothing can change this. To attempt to claim her own power through revenge, Lysiane turns the tables on Robert by claiming Querelle for herself. Conversely, Querelle, by having an affair with Lysiane, claims power over his brother, finally revealing to Lysiane that it is the power play among men that counts, and that women have no place in that power structure. When Lysiane realizes that she has been used as a pawn by Querelle, she confronts him, essentially begging him to reassure her that the play between Querelle and herself as lovers has some meaning. To this entreaty Querelle responds that Lysiane means nothing to him, that she is "just a woman." In making this admission, Querelle implies that the sexual power play between people always comes down to a form of play between men and that the net result of sexual play is denial, betrayal, and negation.

The last few scenes of *Querelle* provide us with a final instance of a sexual game between men that cancels itself. Towards the end of the film, Querelle becomes Lt. Seblon's lover, having shown earlier that he feels contempt, not passion, for the lieutenant. Where earlier Querelle had taken the role of master over the lieutenant by exploiting the latter's infatuation, at the end of the film Querelle willingly surrenders himself to the lieutenant, asking to be taken sexually so that afterwards, Querelle says, the Lieutenant can hold him "like a pietà cradling a small Jesus." In offering himself, however, Querelle commits the ultimate betrayal: openly, ardently begging to be exploited, Querelle has destroyed his own image as a hypermasculine "man's man," confessing that he wants to be transformed into another image, that of the martyred Christ. As he offers himself to the lieutenant, then, Querelle offers himself as an exposed nonentity, caught between poses. Querelle is all image, and the images he presents betray his own emptiness and, by extension, the emptiness of all the images of maleness around him.

I hope the examples we have drawn from the scenes discussed above will indicate how important the trope of doubling is in *Querelle*. Doubling appears in the film to expose the emptiness of sexual games by presenting those games as involving a play between personal identities expressed as images. Within the world of the film, for example, many characters appear or function as doubled images of each other. First, of course, are Querelle and his brother Robert, who do not appear to resemble each other closely but who are characterized by other characters in the film as being doubles of each other. While they do not appear from the viewer's point of view to be twins, Robert and Querelle function as doubles of each other in a number of ways. Both are obsessed with each other, constantly engaged in fierce rivalry; both are regarded by the people around them as real men (hence as doubles of an archetypically male character); both are involved with macho crimes (theft, whoring, violence); and both have an affair with Lysiane. Another set of male doubles in the film, as we have discussed previously, is the set formed by Mario and Nono: two big tough guys who have sex with men and who are frequently seen in the film together, the whoremonger works with the policeman as an informant, and the policeman works with the whoremonger as an accomplice in crime. Gil serves as a double of Querelle (by committing murder) and of Robert (by disguising himself to rob Lt. Seblon). Roger is referred to by Gil as being the double of the former's girlfriend, Paulette (Roger's sister, whom we never see except in photographs). When he is murdered, Vic dies in a paroxysm of ecstasy shot by Fassbinder to resemble a scene of holy martyrdom, thereby presenting a double of Querelle in the latter's humiliation before his brother (during the fight scene) and before Lt. Seblon at the end of the film. And finally, Lt. Seblon functions as a double of Lysiane, of Robert and of Gil, in that all four characters are betrayed by Querelle.

The process of doubling appears in the film also as part of the film's structure. Throughout the film, a visual effect of doubling is attained by highlighting the actors' faces in one of two highly theatrical tones: a nasty yellow-orange or an icy cobalt blue. Often in the film a single character's face is split into two zones of illumination, one side orange and one side blue. Doubling by reversing can be found by comparing the first scene of the film, showing sailors working on board Seblon's ship, with the film's last scene, which presents the same images, played in reverse action.

Another type of doubling involves two scenes in which Mme Lysiane appears. In one scene of the film, Mme Lysiane sits in her boudoir looking into her mirror, talking to her lover Robert, who is on her bed behind her. In another scene later in the film, Lysiane sits in the same fashion, talking with Querelle who has replaced Robert. In both scenes, Lysiane remarks, while looking at her lover's reflected image, that the brothers love only each other, that there is no room for anybody else in their lives.

Often in the film, characters sit looking into mirrors, talking to or about another character, but looking at an image in reflection. As with many of Fassbinder's other films (*Effi Briest* comes particularly to mind here), the people of *Querelle* frequently appear looking not directly at someone else or at their own reflection, but rather at the reflection of another person. Through this gesture, the person looking into the mirror sees and contemplates not another person but rather the image that person presents. What the observing person sees, then, is always a flat image, an image whose flatness contains a truth about the identity of the one being looked at: that the person being observed is nothing more than the image, and that the image then reveals the depthlessness not only of the identity of the one observed but also of the act of observing itself.[6]

All of the various doublings in the film reflect back to the character of Querelle, constructed in the film as a flat image of hypermasculinity, an image that focuses on what Steven Shaviro explains as the presentation of Querelle as a hypermale body:

This body turned image is not an object fantasized or produced by masculine desire so much as it is the lure that arouses and shapes such desire in the first place. As Querelle grows "within us," he imposes himself upon us as the very definition of our desire, the image of what we would like ourselves to have (possession of the image) and to be (identification with the image). The spectator is interpellated as a subject, and gendered male, in the course of his encounter with and seduction by this banal image. The film traces a double dependency, a double passivity: the process

by which the male body is imaged and objectified is concomitant with
that by which it is captivated and subjectified. Both the subject and the
object of the gaze are submitted to the absorptive, derealizing play of the
image.[7]

Following Shaviro's line of thought, Querelle's image, described at one point in
the film as being like that of the Angel of the Apocalypse, serves to announce a
shattering of the meaning behind the male image. When Querelle, the very picture of a hypermale stereotype, is presented before us as objectified through the
eyes of Seblon, Lysiane, Robert Nono, Mario and Gil, he reveals to us that the
purest image of masculinity serves as the locus for the shattering of masculinity:
to be masculine is to look, to be active, yet Querelle exists passively to be
looked at; to be masculine means to desire, and Querelle is desired while he
desires no one. When the film shows Querelle having sex, it shows him having
it only with other men, as a passive participant (while the film's narrator tells us
that, at one point, Querelle becomes Lysiane's lover, we never see them make
love or even embrace). As a stereotypical image of masculinity, then, Querelle
presents what underlies that image as being nothing but sexual passivity.

As the central image of hypermasculinity in the film, Querelle assumes the
role of monster by virtue of his isolation.[8] When, for instance, early in the film
Querelle goes into a bar in Brest, he appears set apart from the scene full of
games playing itself out around him. As Querelle enters the bar, Gil is playing
guitar and Theo, who habitually torments Gil with sexual innuendoes, is playing
an obnoxiously loud video game, the noise apparently meant as an annoyance
for Gil. Dressed, like Gil, in a hypermasculine version of stonemason's garb that
recalls the members of the group Village People in its degree of exaggerated
maleness, the latter stonemason, looks over his shoulder from time to time at
Gil, appearing to "cruise" him. Against this scene suggestive of homoerotic desire, Querelle enters the bar, now looking slightly troubled as he lights a cigarette. As he does this, the film's narrator quotes from Genet: "Querelle was not
used to the idea that he was a monster. A young man, he knew the terror of being alone, caught in the world of the living."

The world of the living as it is here presented to us is a scene of game-
playing between and among men. Theo is playing a video game and in doing so,
is playing a game with Gil by making annoying noises. Gil's playing guitar also
constitutes a game between Roger and himself: the game is one in which Gil
affirms his normal masculinity while he flirts with Roger. Into this constellation
of men walks Querelle, who is alone: he is not actively caught up in a chain of
desire with anyone present. Because he is not part of the loop in which Gil,
Roger and Theo find themselves, Querelle is, at this moment in the film, an aberration, a monstrous anomaly with reference to the norms of interaction that
exist around him. If this line of analysis holds, then through it we can discern
one of the film's most important assumptions: here it is given as normal that
men play transgressive games of desire with each other, while it is presented as

monstrous when a man appears not playing such a game. What makes Querelle monstrous here is that, by standing in isolation, he makes it evident that all the men around him—each of them a "real" man—participate in a transgressive circle of homoerotic desire. As an isolated figure, Querelle exposes the play of desire among other men, and thus he constitutes a sign or *monstrum* exposing a contradiction at the heart of the dominant male order: namely, that in the play of identities among men there is a strong element of desire *between* men.

Near the film's end, when Querelle reveals to Lysiane that he has had sex with Nono, Lysiane tells him "You have mysterious powers—you are not of this earth." In saying this, Lysiane recalls the words the film's narrator speaks in the bar scene discussed immediately above. By exposing the truth to Lysiane, that Querelle the macho man is actually a "fairy," Querelle has broken the most important rule of "this" world: maintain appearances. By breaking the rules, Querelle has exposed himself as a monster, an anomalous creature who stands as a sign, or more accurately, as a portent, that the male order of things "of this earth" is a lie. As Querelle leaves the Feria with the lieutenant, Lysiane reads Robert's cards again, declaring now that he has no brother. Having embraced abjection in the arms of the lieutenant, Querelle has finally effected his self-annihilation, and hence his image no longer exists. Here the narrator's voice comments: "Querelle's harmony was now indestructible, because it was united in that heaven of heavens where beauty unites with beauty." That is, Querelle, by annihilating himself as a real man, by becoming an abjectly monstrous perversion of manhood, has united with the emptiness that underlies his image as a man, and in this emptiness he has found his true identity.

As the film ends, we see a repetition of the scene shown at the beginning of the film—sailors laboring on the deck of the ship—played now in reverse motion, creating a sense in the film, finally, that everything we have seen before in the film has been somehow reversed. What the film has, indeed, reversed is a sense of what is normal and what is aberrant not simply in male identity, but also in the dynamics of pleasure and violence. At the end of the film Querelle, the archetypal image of maleness, becomes the subject of the power and the pleasure of Seblon, the fairy. By doing so, however, Querelle has destroyed the source of Seblon's desire. This fact and the logic of the film as a whole reverse the received logic by which the abject homosexual is located as a powerless deformity on the outside of the patriarchal power structure. Indeed, the film appears to assert that it is the homosexual, as the one who purveys and propagates archetypal images of maleness, who has a central position of power because he defines and disseminates the images by which patriarchy defines itself.

In the final analysis, the character of Querelle discloses a terrible secret concerning masculinity. This secret is that, at the heart of men's search for their own masculinity, there is a desire to be undone, a desire not to affirm identity but rather to surrender it. In the logic of sexual desire, expressing sexual identity means ultimately subjecting oneself to the experience of *ekstasis* or *being driven out of one's senses*. In its purest sense, being thus driven can only mean transgressing or abandoning the limits of identity. By this logic, the search for sexual identity, if it is most faithfully followed, finally leads to a type of self-annihilation: passion most fully expressed makes us *come* completely out of ourselves, and the experience leaves us *spent*. Thus it is in Fassbinder's film that Mme Lysiane says that Querelle "is in danger of finding himself": the prospect of finding one's self means expressing sexual identity, but expressing sexual identity implies the peril of achieving self-annihilation. Thus, in Fassbinder's film, Querelle the consummate transgressor performs the role of sexual monster in that he serves as a sign revealing the secret of the true nature of maleness. That secret is that maleness, finally, is an endless reflection upon itself.

NOTES

1. See in particular, Olivier Assayas, "L'Enfer de Brest," review of *Querelle*, *Cahiers du cinéma*, N340, Oct. 1982: 27-30
2. The name "Feriâ," original to Genet's novel, is a common Spanish word meaning "fair" or "market." Thus the name of the brothel implies the activities of playing and selling.
3. Steven Shaviro, *The Cinematic Body*. Theory Out of Bounds, vol. 2 (Minneapolis: University of Minnesota Press, 1993), 179.
4. In an interview with Kurt Raab, Dieter Schidor discusses the way that Fassbinder's *Querelle* normalizes abnormality:

Kurt: It [the film] is absolutely not a film intended to be sexually arousing for gays?

Schidor: Nope. The film has something totally new. You can barely give it a name. There is something in the films of the fat man [Fassbinder] that makes everything appear so completely taken for granted. A kind of normalcy is what it is. Throughout the whole film you think: All this is normal.

Kurt: What other people call normal has been presented [in Fassbinder's films] as so completely normal, that you take it for granted that this is so?

Schidor: Exactly. The film never says, Look, see how hot it is, the way those two are fucking. Look, how brutal it is, when that one gets murdered. Never. You are never astonished. If it had been shown in an obscene fashion, you would say: The director is obscene. Since Mary [i.e., Fassbinder] was hardly ever astonished at any of the things that astonished other people, she shows them as normal. In the Fuck [*sic*] scenes between Querelle (Brad Davis) and Günther Kaufmann, what she shows is this: that's how it is. It is not vulgar, and nonetheless it leaves room for the thought that [the way the film was shot] could have been taken much further. [My translation.]

See Kurt Raab and Dieter Schidor, "Dialog V," in Kurt Raab and Karsten Peters, *Die Sehnsucht des Rainer Werner Fassbinders* (München: C. Bertelsmann Verlag GmbH: 1982), 335.

5. Jeffrey Malkan, "Aggressive Text: Murder and the Fine Arts Revisited," *Mosaic* (Winnipeg), Winter 1990, v23, n1: 101.

6. In this connection, Steven Shaviro writes:

The typically postmodern self-consciousness of Fassbinder's images—their blatant sound-stage artificiality, their continual doublings and reflections, our sense that they are always already "in quotation marks"—indicates that they cannot be regarded as (more or less adequate) representations: not of Genet's novel, and less of "real life." Fassbinder's Sirkian fondness for mirrors and for overly ornate visual tableaux had never been more in evidence. We quickly come to recognize the play of simulacra: since everything in the film is a reflection, an "imitation of life," "reality" and "life" are entirely exhausted and consumed by artifice, or by commodification. There is no outside reality left to be imitated and reflected. Everything is on the surface, posed for the cameras, bathed in an artificial glow, processed through orange or blue filters. See Shaviro, 167.

7. Shaviro, 175.

8. In an interview in the *Saturday Review,* Günther Schidor, the film's producer and the actor who portrays Vic, observes of the film:

I know some people say the film is about homosexuality, but Fassbinder didn't think that at all. He always said it was not a movie about or on any form of homosexuality but about one person's search for identity, with the rituals of masculinity that happen between men and all the dangers that go with them. These dangers include the breaking of taboos. The main character is at ease with being a monster because he knows the feeling of being alone.

Perhaps unwittingly, Schidor indicates here that the film inscribes monstrosity (in the sense of male sexual deviance) as existing within the order of heterosexual male value as Fassbinder finds it given. Denying, as Fassbinder did, that *Querelle* is "about" homosexuality, Schidor appears to be simultaneously asserting that Fassbinder intends to place Querelle's being a monster firmly within the "normal" order of male values. See Schidor, quoted in Elizabeth Nickles, "Overripe Beauty," in *Saturday Review*, May/June 1983: 20.

CHAPTER 5

Embracing the Queer Monster: Dark Lovers, Wild Lives

Sometimes the queer monster appears in film as a lover, like Cocteau's angel Heurtebise, who comes forth in the life of a gay outsider to fill that life with meaning. Derek Jarman's *Edward II* (1991) takes advantage of this trope to depict gay men living outside the law—living, in fact, in perilous conflict with it. Edward's Gaveston is his muse, the source of inspiration that makes him forget, however briefly, that the world around him is his enemy. But Gaveston is also something of a demon, appearing, in one scene, perched naked like a gargoyle on the throne as he hurls insults at Edward's foes. Gaveston is an intolerable irritant to the world of Edward's court, most clearly because he takes every opportunity to remind its members of their own falseness. Hence he must be done away with, and his death makes Edward's fall a certainty. Jarman presents all the gay men of this film as somewhat monstrous. They are often covered with dirt or blood in a visual suggestion that we are seeing them through the eyes of the world around them, the world that wants them gone.

Another dark lover appears in Patrice Chéreau's *L'Homme blessé* (*The Wounded Man*, 1983) in which a young, working-class man discovers his homosexuality when he is thrown together with an imposing street hustler. As the young man becomes drawn into an obsession with the older man, he moves ever closer to madness, finally realizing his passion as he kills and then embraces the object of his desire. Agustin Villaronga's *Tras El Cristal* (*In a Glass Cage*, 1986) presents a young survivor of Nazi sex torture—a beautiful young gamin—who turns the tables on his tormentor to act out the role of sexual dominator. In *Les nuits sauvages* (*Savage Nights*, 1993) a handsome bisexual man in the final stages of AIDS—played by the film's director and writer, Cyril Collard, in a recreation of events of his own life—splits his intimate life between a rather too sweetly romantic, unsafe encounter with a naive young girl and grimly realistic, wildly passionate sessions of anonymous public sex with other men.

These dark lovers all force us—especially gay men—to look into all that is most hated about being gay and face it squarely: the attack on "Nature," the violence of passion, the dirty fascination with semen and piss and shit—in short, all the terror that our culture feels about maleness—and recognize that underlying that terror is fear of and disgust towards physical bodies.

Tom Kalin's *Swoon* (1992) presents two gay monsters caught up in the mess of their own passions, passions that eventually overwhelm them. The film invites us to do two things: to ask what causes these two men, Richard Loeb (portrayed by Daniel Schlachet) and Nathan Leopold (portrayed by Craig Chester), to commit a senseless crime; and to see the murderers as being engaging characters. By making them appear more beautiful than handsome, for one thing, Kalin makes us see each of them through the eyes of the other. We see them as if we were their lovers. Kalin's camera relentlessly shows them up close and ready to kiss, looking at them—two of this century's most notorious killers, no less—as they agonize their way through finding a way out of a society in which they've already lost from the start (they're Jewish and gay). The way out leads them into crimes that let them forget being Jewish, first of all, and being homos, secondly—which ironically leads the one survivor back to the Kaddish, the prayer for the dead. Significantly, the bits we hear translated from the Kaddish focus on reconciliation between humankind and the universe. And that, perhaps, is the only consolation this horribly dark film offers—a prayer for reconciliation.

Shot in grainy black and white, the film casts everything in it in a mode of fashion magazine glamour, presenting Loeb and Leopold as two elegant young men smitten as much by anomie as by each other. What makes these elegant young men different from those one finds in forties film noir is that Kalin's film consistently keeps the viewer close to them, both by using frequent close-ups and by suggesting, in the highly stylized look of the film, their very point of view. The film seeks further to bring us closer to the principal characters by violating the integrity of the film's world as constructed fiction. Recreating the historical period of twenties in a conventional way (using costumes and set design), Kalin's film matter-of-factly dispenses with that reconstruction in a number of small ways. For instance, often as we see Loeb and Leopold talking with each other on the telephone, we note with some astonishment that they are using

Touch-Tone phones. Furthermore, at one point in the film Kalin inserts a documentary-style treatise on perversion, featuring still shots of people in (for the audience) contemporary clothing and appearance. The message behind the documentary section is that everybody is a pervert, hence that all of us are proximate to Loeb and Leopold in the murkiness of our passions, the darkness of our appetites.

Kalin's film contrasts the madness of his two principal characters with that of normal men, depicted as a form of mythomania that must invent stories to explain everything. It doesn't make sense to try to account for a brutal murder of a child by saying the murderers did the deed because they were obsessed with penises in general and their own in particular, but that doesn't stop the gentlemen of the court from trying, and that is what Kalin shows us. It's the order of things that's obsessed with penises in *Swoon*; certainly Loeb and Leopold are obsessed, but their obsession is never quite apprehended by the people around them, and that is their real agony as we see them. They agonize mainly over their crimes in terms of logistics—details, details, all in a day's work, but what a bother! Their real agony is a form of spiritual emptiness that the film doesn't allow to be reduced to a matter of men desiring other men; its true nature, this anomie, is one of impenetrable isolation, indecipherable pain, which the two men hide from the rest of the world by their elegance, their refusal to be understood even as they proclaim themselves to the world during their trial.

There is no easy answer to their crimes, and perhaps that is precisely why the world of the court needs so much to find one. They're fags, that's all: that's why they did it, that's the only way to account for such a crime. Nathan gives his interrogators the one clue that might help them understand the mystery of the murder a little better. In a throwaway admission as he is being interrogated, he tells the police that he had chosen Bobby Frank simply at random—thus admitting that his crime is not to be understood rationally. And yet the police take that admission and do nothing with it, attempting instead to push through the facts and mold them into a "clear" understanding of what made these two men kill. It won't work, figuring out such a crime: its very nature calls for admitting the impotence of rationality before certain types of violence, and that cannot be admitted.

Kalin essentially presents Loeb and Leopold as signal characters, as signs for what happens to crazy people who happen to be gay, particularly what happens to them under the influence of a perverted, popularized form of Freudian psychology—in effect, as the film presents it, enclosing all people within the prison of psychopathology. Hence the mugshot scene of the film, in which a succession of diverse strangers are presented in a pseudo-rationalist scheme of pathology—suggesting, essentially, that the conclusion of rationalism via paperback Freudian thought is that everybody is sick, everybody is condemned to a state of criminality more or less the same as are the admitted child murderers. Thus the film suggests that all of us are as subject to our own mad passions as the twisted intellectual perverts who deliberately, by their own unrepentant admission, sought to distance themselves from the "natural" order of things. Both Loeb and Leopold deny their Jewishness, both of them intentionally dive into a life of depravity in the hope, as Nathan says after the child murder, of dealing with their own awareness of their condition: "I wanted to murder the idea of suffering as my condition. I wanted to surpass the boundaries of intelligence for something more pure." Sneakily the film presents us with these two very alien creatures, manages to make—certainly a queer audience—feel sympathy for them, even as we realize the horror of the fact that we are being made to feel kindly towards a pair of cold-blooded murderers. Only after having lured us into feeling for these characters does the film then quietly, simply assert that we the audience are in the same boat as Loeb and Leopold: we've all already been convicted and imprisoned by a culture of judges and juries turning the notion of reason into a monstrous tool for telling lies, lies aimed ultimately at controlling and containing.

Structures of power are presented in the film as replicating themselves and in this series of replications the film permits us to follow a tracking of the line of confusion by which the powerful in our society link sexuality with morality. The film asserts that the great injustice done to Loeb and Leopold was done during their sensational trial, a trial in which the prosecution built its case around the idea that Loeb and Leopold had sexually abused their young victim at some point during the murder. Furthermore, the prosecution is presented as having methodically used the sexual nature of Nathan's and Dick's relationship to support the contention that theirs was a particularly horrible crime: it wasn't just a crime, it was a murder; it wasn't just a murder, it was a child murder; it wasn't just a child murder, it was a child murder that involved homosexual activity, both between the perpetrators and between the perpetrators and the young victim. At the same time, the film presents defense lawyer Clarence Darrow (played by Robert Read) arguing vehemently that because their homosexuality was, of necessity, a sickness, Dick and Nathan could not be held accountable for their crime; in other words, the fact that they were homosexual was full and sufficient proof that they were insane. On both sides of the court, then, the argument was made that understanding their homosexuality was fundamental to understanding their criminal actions. The absurdity of this position, through which one side could then argue that their homosexuality made them ineluctably guilty while the other side argued that it unmistakably proved them non compos mentis, is underscored by the fantasy scene in which Dick and Nathan are depicted as having sex on a huge bed in the middle of the courtroom while the courtroom audience sits politely looking towards the bench, not seeming to notice all the carryings-on. As the film presents the story, the accusation that the murderers' sexuality had anything to do with their crime is exposed clearly as a lie. The film's audience is made to see, then, what the audience of the court did not see: that the situation into which Loeb and Leopold were placed by the trial was essentially one of being victimized by the law's homophobia. Dick and Nathan were monsters, but not because they were gay.

Kalin seems to have chosen the story because it provides so many details about the nature of justice for gay people. After all, Loeb and Leopold confessed their crime even before the trial began, which meant that the whole point of the trial was to determine not whether something had happened, but rather, What was the nature of this crime, and how was it then to be punished? The answer that the trial gives is that it is because these men were homosexual that their crime was particularly outrageous. Ironically, what was lost in this judgement was a true sense of what was lost in the murder of Bobby Frank: Did the murder of a child really need to be given a special weight (by proving the monstrousness of the murderers) to justify punishment for it?

What the audience is encouraged to see, because our seeing is linked with the points of view of Loeb and Leopold, is that their pathology was not congruent with their sexuality. Their sexuality was complex, driven by ritual and sadomasochism—hence the very theatrical vignettes in which we see several characters reading from Sacher-Masoch's *Venus in Furs*, echoing the erotic play of master and slave between Nathan, the supposed master, and Dick, the supposed slave. Just as their sexuality was frankly depicted as having a strongly dark element, however, it was also characterized in the film by unquestionably real tenderness and passion. We are encouraged by the film to see their sexuality as consensual and complex, certainly as well developed—not infantile—but rather defying clear evaluation. What then do we do with their crime spree? They didn't just commit a murder, after all; they committed a number of crimes, starting small and ending up with the murder of a randomly chosen young boy. Or was their last crime actually their betrayal of each other under the pressure of interrogation?

Without giving us a clear answer to how we might do so, the film undermines the legitimacy of attempting to connect Loeb and Leopold's sexuality with their crime, and then leaves open to us how we might understand what made these young men become murderers. We are invited to see them as social monsters—they are unusually engaging villains, and hence even more unusual as gay cinematic characters—and yet preserve a sense that the evil they did was not fully congruent with the people they were. We are most clearly invited by this film to separate what we know about them as sexual beings from what we know about them as social misfits. The two men were monsters, not by virtue of their sexuality, but rather by virtue of a social void that existed within them.

Criminality and homosexuality are issues treated by another filmmaker, Todd Haynes. In fact, by the time Haynes presented his film *Poison* at the Sundance Film Festival in 1991, he had already become notorious as a maker of dangerous films. His film *Superstar: The Karen Carpenter Story*, a forty-three-minute feature first shown in 1989, depicted the rise and fall of singer Karen Carpenter in what quickly became viewed as a controversial, if not downright tasteless, fashion. Because, in his film, Haynes had used music whose copyrights were controlled by Ms. Carpenter's heirs, he was subjected to a lawsuit by Ms. Carpenter's family, which action ultimately led to the film's being legally banned from distribution and exhibition.[1] *Superstar* featured a stylistic mixture of documentary-style fragments and fictional narrative, both of which complemented each other in the way they treated the film's central point of concern: the link between the idealization of women's bodies and eating disorders. What made the film so disturbing (and makes it still so powerful) was the fact that the fictional narrative section of the film was acted out with Barbie and Ken dolls manipulated in live action on a miniature set. This choice effects in the film something extraordinary: a simultaneous diminution and enlargement of the character we see before us. Portrayed as a stiffly moving, crudely deformed doll hooked on Ex-Lax, the Karen Carpenter of Haynes's film is, at one and the same time, a comically reduced visual cliché (a pre-packaged simulacrum of femininity) and a tragically enlarged voice—the voice of a woman who, ironically, made her living by sounding smoothly beautiful just as she slowly slid towards death because no one could (or would) hear her.

The violence of Haynes's style in *Superstar* thus condemned the film to becoming a piece of outlaw art: to this day, the film cannot be exhibited legally. The supreme irony here is that Haynes's film does not appear to be a hateful bit of libel leveled against Ms. Carpenter; if anything, it is an indictment against a culture that hates women. Because the legal case against Superstar has been closed, however, the film currently enjoys a peculiar status among American films. Having been legally barred from distribution, it now circulates among a criminal underground of copyright violators who distribute bootleg copies on videocassette to a small but eager criminal audience. Ironically, by wresting control of the film from its maker, the powers working against *Superstar* have only served to enlarge and deepen the subversive nature of its appearance.

It was thus against the background of the furor over Superstar that Todd Haynes took *Poison* to the Sundance Film Festival, where he got into more trouble. *Poison*, which was funded in part by a grant from the National Endowment for the Arts, featured, among other things, badly behaving homosexual characters, the erotic fantasies of children, and a scene excerpted from Genet's *Miracle of the Rose* in which several male, adolescent prisoners sexually taunt another boy by spitting on him repeatedly. At the screening at Sundance, viewers walked out in protest during the spitting scene. During the highly publicized media furor that ensued following the film's first few screenings, Senator Jesse Helms held up the film as an example of the NEA's "elitist" excesses in passing pornography as art at taxpayers' expense, and the ultraconservative Rev. Donald Wildmon excoriated the film as being "homosexual pornography" without ever having actually viewed it.[2] Furthermore, it was reported in the press that White House Chief of Staff John Sununu used the occasion of the controversy surrounding the film to compromise the leadership of the National Endowment for the Arts under John Frohnmayer, and in fact, Frohnmayer resigned his post not long after the *Poison* scandal subsided.[3]

As Haynes himself has observed, *Superstar* and *Poison* are of a piece with each other in that they both explore the stylistic mixture of cinematic tropes. In *Superstar* Haynes mixes documentary and fictional narrative to force the viewer to retain a level of critical awareness while viewing the film. By mixing cinematic styles as he does in *Superstar*, Haynes obliges the viewer to refrain from settling into a position of simply enjoying the wickedness of an abusively drawn story (big trouble at Barbie's house) to realize that the story is not merely about laughing at little, false creatures, but that rather it is far more about the enormity of smallness and falseness among real people. In *Poison* Haynes takes the idea of mixing cinematic tropes at least one major step further: he does this by mixing documentary style with narrative fictional style, and by joining those two styles to a pastiche of genre cinema—the horror film.

Commenting on the central problem of *Poison*, Haynes notes how the film places homosexuality in the context of a larger social issue, namely that of understanding deviance and normalcy: "With homosexuality and my films I don't know that in *Poison* there is evidence for arguments of essential difference in homosexuality. Instead there is an attempt to link homosexuality to other forms that society is threatened by—deviance that threatens the status quo or our sense of what normalcy is."[4] If the issue of *Poison* is looking at the threat that deviance poses to society, then the strategy by which the film discusses the issue is one of linking forms of deviance together to show both how variously deviance can be seen and how, at a fundamental level, all forms of deviance converge in the way they mark the person who is seen as deviant. The mark that is performed upon deviant people, the film suggests, is one through which the deviant becomes identified by society as an outsider, as a social or physical monster. Once the deviant individual is so marked, he is unalterably doomed, and the logic of the film, as Haynes has noted, comes to organize itself around a triptych depicting "how society poisons all of us no matter how fully we choose to participate in its rules and regulations."[5]

Poison is arranged as three interlocking stories, titled "Horror," "Hero," and "Homo," which present three central male characters, each of whom exhibits a certain form of deviance. This status as deviant is coded somewhat differently for each of them, but what is common to all is that their deviance is linked with some sort of sexual monstrousness. For each of these three characters, monstrousness is linked to a perverse type of dreaming. Dr. Thomas Graves, the central character of "Horror," is a man who, obsessed from early childhood with the idea of making history by making a breakthrough in medical research, realizes his dream as a young doctor when he manages to isolate the essence of the human sex drive as a chemical distillate. The dream goes sour, however, when the handsome Dr. Graves accidentally drinks the distillate, which turns him into a grotesquely deformed, lethally contagious, sex-killing leper. Richie Beacon, the boy who is the central character of "Hero" (and who never appears fully on screen), is presented variously by witness testimony as being either a prodigy or a pervert. Like Dr. Graves, Richie has his own personal dreams, but for Richie, these dreams occur as fantastic stories that emerge from his own imagination. Much of Richie's dreaming involves sadomasochistic fantasies.[6] Richie realizes one of his dreams by acting out one of these stories: in it he saves his mother's life by killing his abusive father, after which he miraculously flies away, never to be seen again. And John Broom, the repeat-offender prison convict who is the central character of "Homo," realizes his own erotic dream by playing out a sadomasochistic pursuit with the object of his obsession, the prisoner Jack Bolton.

The film begins by presenting establishing shots that occur as fragments of each of the three stories, each fragment briefly introducing a central character and then abruptly cutting into the next, so that from the very beginning, the viewer is prevented from settling into any comfortable sense of knowing who the film is centrally about. The only clue we get, at the beginning of the film, that there might be something that ties these three evidently very different stories together is an acknowledgment we see as the introductory film credits roll: namely, that the film contains excerpts from Genet's *Miracle of the Rose, Our Lady of the Flowers*, and *Thief's Journal*. This acknowledgment leads us at first to believe that, with the three stories of the film, perhaps we are to get some sort of alignment with the three Genet novels. But it soon becomes clear, that in the way Haynes links the fragments of the stories he has created and the excerpts he has taken from Genet, he is challenging the viewer, as Justin Hyatt says, "to seek connections and resonances between each story and its characters: between the enigmatic child Richie Beacon, the alienated scientist Dr. Graves, and the resolute prisoner John Broom."[7] As part of the strategy Haynes employs to lead us to see these resonances, he includes lines from each of the three Genet novels in each of the three stories, with the greatest number of excerpts from Genet appearing in the "Homo" section of the film, which is largely constructed out of fragments from *Miracle of the Rose* (most notably, the infamous spitting scene) and *Thief's Journal*. In fact, the name of the character John Broom, the central character of "Homo," is a translation of "Jean Genet," as we learn when we read in *Thief's Journal* that "the very day he met me [Genet] Jean Cocteau called me 'his Spanish genêt' (genêt d'Espagne)—rush-leaved broom."[8]

Just as the film resolutely prevents us from deciding who the film is most centrally about, it obliges us, instead, to abandon this question fairly early on by providing links between each story on a number of levels, the various links serving to ask us: What is it that cuts across all three stories? What we find as we go on in the film is not a neat compartmentalization of fragments taken from one Genet novel and inserted consistently into a single story within the film, but rather something of a cut up effect in which different fragments from all three novels appear unevenly distributed throughout the film. Certainly, as noted above, the section of the film that presents the longest, most coherent block from Genet's writings is the "Homo" section of the film; but this section does not simply adapt *Thief's Journal* or *Miracle of the Rose*; it includes fragments from all three of Genet's novels, extrapolated by Haynes to include the character of Jack Bolton, the object of John Broom's desire. Furthermore, Haynes links the three stories together, as Nicholas Jenkins has noted,

> by a dense web of visual rhymes and narrative echoes: the hands of the young thief Bolton [sic] sliding through his foster parents' drawers are picked up in the image of Richie's fingers groping around in the dark for his father's revolver; the two rounds he pumps into his parent's body resound as the shots that bring down Bolton as he tries to escape from prison.[9]

What is most striking about the various devices of resonance that the film presents is how they all seem to point towards an identification between sexual deviance, imprisonment (either literal, as in John Broom's case, or figurative, as in Richie's and John Graves's case), violence, abjection and ecstasy. As we have already seen from our discussion of *A Song of Love* and *Querelle*, the Genetic connection between these phenomena tends finally to embrace this process of identification as affirming the glory of the homosexual monster—abjection in its most rarefied state mutating, by the force of a phase change, into apotheosis. With Haynes, however, this identification appears to be ironic: that is, while Haynes seems to partake of Genet's sense that there is something deeply beautiful in abjection, he does seem, in the final analysis, to indicate that the identification between all the factors that lead to abjection and ecstasy represents, for his three monstrous characters, a state of loss.

If we see the film's thematic dynamic in this way, we are ultimately led to see Haynes as using Genet's notion of abjection not simply as a queer appropriation of monstrosity. More than that, Haynes appears to be delivering a defiant critique that, having embraced the idea that queers (and, we must remember, other deviants as well) are monsters in the view of the status quo, invites queer people to see and claim the strength inherent to accepting that one is a monster. Having done that, one must then go on and create something truly affirmative out of that acceptance. *Poison* does not simply invite queer people to identify with Dr. Graves, Richie or John Broom. It invites us to take the strength of character implicit in their monstrous natures and use it to fight the status quo. Thus where Genet would have said that he would not wish that world to change so that he could always be against it, Haynes, I think, would say that he would be against the status quo to make it change, under the creative force of the deviant, so that deviance would no longer be linked to abjection.

The fragments in *Poison* taken from Genet constitute a varied set of elements that function in a number of ways throughout the film. One way these fragments appear in the film is as single lines spoken by a character. For example, close to the end of the film, when Dr. Graves lies dying, we hear him say, as his last words, a line taken from *Our Lady of the Flowers*: "I hear angels farting on the ceiling." The line is wickedly ironic in the context we find it in the film—the mad doctor, finally brought into the protective custody of an emergency room after flinging himself from a window into the mob that has pursued him, has a chance to utter a final benediction, a final resolution to the disorder he has precipitated with his perverse work. As he lies dying, the eager doctors try to comfort him and, expecting him to use his dying breath to come back into the fold of normalcy—by contritely, gracefully renouncing his crime—they are met instead by an inscrutable utterance, a slightly indecent epitaph that seals his fate: he dies beyond the pale. As he dies, we see flickering images of an ancient angel: it is the angel of Garcia Márquez's "A Very Old Man With Enormous Wings," at one and the same time a shocking and a comically diminished image of salvation. As he dies, then, Graves reinscribes his monstrosity upon the order of things by uttering what sounds like nonsense, thereby emphasizing the absurdity of the idea of being brought back into the fold of normalcy.

Another way in which fragments from Genet appear in the film is as intertitles placed between blocks of action. At one point in the "Homo" section of the film, John Broom, who has had a decades-long obsession with the prisoner Jack Bolton, has fallen asleep beside Bolton. We know from what has come before in the film that John is openly aware of his homosexuality and that he embraces it as part of what makes him a criminal. To Broom, embracing criminality and embracing homosexuality within criminality enable him to live in a perverse priesthood that centers around a celebration of men living exclusively among men. The rites of this priesthood are acts of violence, transgressive sex and betrayal. Bolton tells us of his obsession with Jack Bolton, which serves in the film as the most focused expression of his devotion within the prison "priesthood," that whenever he imagines his life with Jack, he always imagines it ending violently. In the odd logic of prison life, John is able to admit openly to a prison warder that he is homosexual, but as we see him move among the other prisoners, we know that it is part of the game men play among each other there to deny being queer. Admitting that one is queer in prison would be a violation of the code of honor—honor among thieves—that requires anyone to win and retain the badge of manhood by declaring again and again that he is a "real" man and not a fairy. For his own part, Jack is unable to admit his own erotic attraction to other men—especially other criminals—despite the fact that he betrays that attraction with virtually every word he speaks, every action he commits. Because he is "closeted," then, and because, in the world of the prison, nothing is more shameful among the criminals (most of whom seem to be fully engaged in an erotic attraction to one another) than admitting one's homosexuality, Jack arouses John further by challenging him, unconsciously, to betray himself. In order to embrace his love for Jack, then, John must betray himself if he is to seek sexual release. Thus, in the scene in which John and Jack are sleeping beside each other, we see John wake up and give in to temptation: he begins stroking Jack's sleeping body, and we see the gentle pleasure on his face that comes from finally having contact with the object of his desire. As the camera shows John begin dreamily to fondle Jack's erect penis, we hear a noise in the background that causes Jack to awaken. As he rouses himself, Jack grabs but does not remove John's hand, and we see the following intertitle, a quotation from *Our Lady of the Flowers*: "My heart's in my hand, and my hand is pierced, and my hand's in the bag, and the bag is shut, and my heart is caught." The intertitle serves to comment here on the nature not merely of the specific acts we have just seen, but more importantly, on the nature of desire. John's desire betrays him as soon as he expresses it. When he finally gives in to the need to seek tenderness with another man, he effectively strips himself bare by revealing that he is a fairy, not a real man. Literally imprisoned in an environment—and here, I think, the prison environment can clearly be seen as standing in for the structure of "normal" male relationships—that denies tenderness and desire among men, John is caught as he gives the lie to that denial. Having given into his desire has involved his committing an act of violence: against Jack by essentially molesting him, and against himself by revealing the truth of his desire. Desire, then, equals violence and betrayal. By expressing his desire, John places himself in a prison within a prison: he is the criminal outcast who has broken the law of prison life. By betraying himself as he gives in to his desire, then, John marks himself as a monster within the convicts' framework of value: having betrayed the code of conduct of the prison, he has executed a sign that the code itself is a lie.

The third and most significant way that fragments from Genet's novels appear in the film occurs as scenes adapted directly from Genet. The most extended such adaptation is the scene from *Miracle of the Rose* in which the inmates of a boys' prison spit on one of their fellow inmates. In Genet's novel, the scene follows the novel's main character, who is Genet himself, as he remembers how one of his former fellow inmates, a boy named Divers, taunted him by recounting how another prisoner, Bulkaen, with whom Jean had been infatuated, had been humiliated by a group of prisoners that included Divers himself. Divers recounts this scene of humiliation, Jean tells us in the novel, to tease Jean about his infatuation. Divers then recounts how one day the boys of the prison cornered Bulkaen and forced him to stand still with his mouth open as the group of tormentors repeatedly spat onto his face and into his mouth. The abuse comes to an end, however, when one of the boys notices that Bulkaen, virtually soaked from head to toe with mucus, has an erection. Imagining this scene, Jean tells us that

a trifle would have sufficed for the ghastly game to be transformed into a courtly one and for me to be covered not with spit but with roses that had been tossed at me. For as the gestures were the same, it would not have been hard for destiny to change everything: the game is organized... youngsters make the gesture of hurling... it would cost no more for them to hurl happiness. We were in the middle of the most flowery park in France. I waited for roses. I prayed God to alter his intention just a little, to make false movement so that the children, ceasing to hate me, would love me. They would have gone on with the game... but with their hands full of flowers, for it would have taken so little for love to enter Van Roy's heart instead of hate.[10]

The sense this scene evokes, so common to Genet's writings, is one of the transubstantiation of an act of violence into one of adoration. What is most important to the thought process by which the Jean Genet of the novel thinks this transubstantiation is a realization of the proximity between violence and love. The realization of this proximity is the moment in which the monster glorifies in his monstrosity, the moment in which he wills his monstrous condition into one of beatification. At this moment, he is the most dangerous creature he can be: he has erased the distance between corruption and sanctification, and in so doing, he has, in effect, escaped from the prison in which being labeled a deviant has placed him.

As realized in the film, the spitting scene represents a memory that Broom has of Bolton. This memory is one of several that we, as viewers, witness from Broom's point of view, contrasting in visual style with the scenes we see of Broom and Bolton together in the film's present time. When we see one of Broom's memories of Bolton, what we see is a scene constructed in terms of highly stylized, decidedly "rosy" color. These scenes are also clearly shot in a studio, so that, though they depict exterior scenes shot on the grounds of a boy's prison, the details of set decoration and lighting clearly lend an artificial quality to them that recalls the luridly set-bound atmosphere of *Querelle*.

The effect of this studio-bound character is to render Broom's memories as having an idealized, oneiric quality that links them to the film's other dreams. Like Broom's dreamy memories of Bolton, John Graves' dream-turned-nightmare is visually coded as a dream through the use of stylized, McCarthy-era horror movie visual tropes: low camera angles, shots using fish-eye lenses that distort facial features, and the use of crisp black and white film print to add an icy touch to all we see of Dr. Graves's decline and fall. Richie's dream vision is similarly coded through a peculiar mixture of devices. In a device recalling "reality television" recreations of real-life events, we see the camera move, during some of the fragments recalling Richie's story, as if it were taking the position of what Richie would have seen as he reacted subjectively to his parents' violent conflict. In other of the Richie Beacon fragments, such as the one in which Richie discovers his mother in bed with the family's gardener, the camera unceremoniously releases itself from a documentary stance to present a very stylized, highly distorted image of action that we can still recognize as being a representation of what Richie is seeing, presented for us as the erotically charged dream-images of a deviant child.

To return to the scene depicting Broom's memory of Bolton's ritual humiliation, what we find in this scene—in my view, the central scene of the film—is a powerful, if certainly disturbing, treatment of homosexuality as monstrosity in the film. It is important to remember in what connection this scene appears in the film. In the scene immediately preceding the spitting scene, Broom, overcome by his long-held desire for Bolton, finds Bolton in a dark hallway of the prison (this scene taking place in the film's present time). Finding Bolton, Broom brutally rapes him, declaring, after he finishes, that he has finally possessed Bolton. Immediately following this violent union, we witness Broom's reminiscence of Bolton's humiliation as a boy: watching from a distance, Broom had watched as a group of boys in the Fontenelle prison had forced Bolton to stand with his mouth open as they took turns spitting on him until he was covered with slime. Seen from the young Broom's point of view, Bolton's face, the beautiful face of a frightened boy, becomes grotesquely, monstrously overlaid with a layer of oozing mucus, recalling Dr. Graves's oozing sores and oddly suggesting Richie's never-seen boy face. As we witness Bolton's facial deformation through Broom's eyes, however, we see John undergo a transfiguration at the lowest point of his abjection: singled out, stripped bare of dignity, exposed by the taunting boys as a "pussy," John suddenly becomes washed by a gentle, heavenly shower of rose petals: the monster, the terrible image of the failure of deviance, is transformed into an image of saintly blessedness.

Appearing near the film's end, the spitting scene is followed by scenes that link the film's three main characters with some version of transfiguration: for Dr. Graves, a ghastly death accompanied by an ironically angelic vision; for Richie Beacon, a miraculous flight in which Richie himself becomes an angelic creature; and for Bolton himself, death during a prison escape attempt, through which end he becomes reified in Broom's mind—it is Broom's face we see as Bolton tries to escape and is killed—as a perfected image of the violence of manly desire, the perfection showing in Jack's perversely beatific face as we last see him, contemplating John's violent end. Through each of these transfigurations, we see a process by which "the 'deviants' in all three stories have achieved a kind of grandeur through their degradations, but [in which] they also perpetuate and deepen the cycles of misery."[11] The misery indicated here is the result of "one of the most fundamental and cynical motives of late-capitalist culture: the construction of a social environment where dissent is discouraged, sensual pleasures are denied, and conformity is rewarded."[12] Thus the three monsters of the film—Dr. Graves, Richie Beacon, and Jack Bolton—serve at last to demonstrate that it is not the deviant who is perverse, but the society that creates him.

Like Haynes's film, Steve McLean's 1994 film, *Postcards from America*, is based on the writings of a fiercely gay writer, David Wojnarowicz. Like Haynes's film, *Postcards* presents a disturbingly fragmented narrative composed of three interweaving threads: images of recollection from three periods in the life of a gay man, never named in the film but named in the credits as David, who survived abuse at every level to come somehow to survive in the midst of an apocalyptic American scene: the world of urban decay, the world of the AIDS pandemic. Also like Haynes's film, *Postcards* focuses attention on the point of view of a character that most of the world would prefer not to have to look at: a deeply troubled gay man who is a drifter and a prostitute. The images we get of this character and from his point of view oblige us to come away from the film with a sense, much like that which Haynes's film creates, that if this nameless character is a sort of social monster—petty criminal, hustler, social outcast—his character as a monster is something the world around him has created. More than that, McLean's film gives us a sense that the nameless man whose life we see played out before us in intercutting memories is a great deal more than the sum of all his wounds and all his crimes. All the terrible things that have happened to David, the film suggests, cannot touch something within him that remains innocent, something that remains pure and alive and deeply, touchingly human.

The film plays out really as a series of vignettes that intercut among one another, each one reflecting through words or images events in the life of the character David at three stages in his life: pre-adolescent boyhood, adolescence, and mature manhood. Portrayed by three different actors, the part of David presents us with a complex image of the identity of a gay man who has lived, virtually since birth, as an outsider. In the vignettes that show us David as a boy, we see how his family life created for him an experience of the world that said, from start to finish, to be a man means to be violent, ruled by lust and thus impotent, unable to connect with anyone who might offer him comfort or for whom he might be a source of uncomplicated love. In these scenes, we see the major events that lead to David's family's disintegration, culminating in his father's committing suicide on Christmas Day one unnamed year. In the violence that characterizes the relationship between David's father and mother, in the great anger and hunger for intimacy that expresses itself as David's father seeking sex from his wife and, it is suggested, even from David, we see the young man managing, miraculously, not to surrender his humanity. Even as we see young David tortured by other neighborhood boys, most of whom seem to be smitten with the same appetite for lust and violence as his father, we see him stealthily figuring out how to fight back, how to refuse to submit to being a victim. Fortunately, young David manages to form a warm, if not homoerotic, relationship with another boy, pictured in scenes in which the two boys are playing just like any kids might, enjoying swimming and each others' company.

The stealth and perseverance that David develops as a child is revealed to us, in the scenes in which David is a teenager, as having taken a much sadder edge. Having survived the violence of his family, the adolescent David has become a street hustler, a hauntingly winsome young man who has learned to live on the streets of New York, supported and provided with company by other outcast kids—principally another young hustler who survived an excruciatingly abusive childhood and a drag queen who provides a shabby but safe little queer hideaway where David can talk and be heard without fearing anything. The world outside this tiny haven is decidedly male and, for the most part, as violent and hurtful as the excesses David suffered at his father's hands. Following David at this point of his life, we see him repeatedly abused and continually thwarted in his attempts to find some way of being in the world that allows him to feel both safe and connected with other people. Occasionally we see the adolescent young man connecting with someone who doesn't want to hurt him— one of David's johns, for instance, is a kindly middle-aged, closeted lawyer who develops an avuncular relationship with the young man. This relationship, however, lasts only awhile. We hear David telling us that this source of warmth in his life simply fell apart at some point, suggesting that perhaps the young man himself, so used to expecting nothing good to last, had been prevented by the violence of his own past from believing that as a young man he could or should take charge of nurturing a relationship based on unconditional love or affection. In the absence of an ability to believe he has a right to be genuinely cared for by other people, the adolescent David moves erratically through his life, like Mike in *My Own Private Idaho*, buffeted by circumstance, generally left, after a violent encounter with another man, hurt and alone.

The adult David, portrayed by James Lyons (the multitalented partner of Todd Haynes), handsome in a painfully melancholy way, appears as the sadly childlike presence surveying his life through recollections of the other two Davids who occupy his past. Burdened by the inability to make peace with this past, the adult David surveys his life as a series of fragments—epitomized in the image of David as an adult, wandering about in a desert—that refuse to come together just as they refuse to allow him to ignore them. It is the adult David whom we see at the beginning and end of the film, caught along the way in scenes that cut with images of his earlier life, his three faces caught in snapshots that record the threads of meaning that have woven themselves throughout his life: life is pain, love is impossible, intimacy means anonymous sex on the run. In the one piece of evidence the film gives us that David had, as an adult, finally found more substantial contact in the form of love with another man, that contact appears before us as already falling apart. In these brief scenes, we see David at the bedside of his lover, who is dying of AIDS, unable to do anything except feel pain and try to push the world away. When we last see David at the end of the film, he is sitting alone in a desert landscape, talking to his now dead lover, telling him with truly heart-breaking eloquence simply how much he wishes the two of them could be fully connected with each other, physically fused and spiritually united in a vision of utter peace.

This painfully beautiful film engages us to see the character of David in the fullness of his complexity. Where, perhaps, we would tend in real life simply to look at a person like David and dismiss him simply as being a human failure or even a social menace, McLean makes us look through the pain of David's experience to see that that pain never manages to conceal what lies deeper. David is not equivalent with his wounds as an abused child or young man, nor is he equivalent with his crimes as a social outlaw. David is not just a hustler, he is a human being who finally shows us that he can speak clearly and movingly about his own need simply to be human—simply to be fully alive and to know another person. After all the horror he has suffered, David finally appears before us articulating, in the language of natural, unrehearsed poetry, his own need for tenderness and for a full connection with his beloved, and in doing this, he appears before us a person whose soul is exposed and illuminated. As we see this character thus brought into the light of recognition, we are obliged to give up thinking that a person such as he is other than us and to see in the petty criminal, the social monster, a good deal of what is most enduring about humanity.

NOTES

1. Caryn James, "Politics nurtures *Poison.* (Todd Haynes' Film Spurs Controversy)," Review of *Poison, The New York Times*, National Edition, 14 April, v.1991, v140, Sec. 2: H15.

2. Maurice Berger, "Todd Haynes' *Poison*," Review of *Poison, Artforum*, October 1991, v30, n2: 17.

3. Richard Corliss, Review of *Poison, Time*, 13 May v1991, v137, n19: 69.

4. Todd Haynes, quoted in Justin Wyatt, "Cinematic/Sexual Transgression: An Interview with Todd Haynes," *Film Quarterly*, v46 N3, Spring 1993: 6.

5. Todd Haynes, quoted in John Anderson, "The Final Cut," Review of *Poison, New York Newsday*, 4 April 1991: 73.

6. Randy Pitman, Review of *Poison. Library Journal.* July 1992, v117, n12: 144.

7. Hyatt, 3.

8. Jean Genet, *The Thief's Journal*, trans. Bernard Frechtman (New York: Grove Press, 1964), 45.

9. Nicholas Jenkins, Review of *Poison, Times Literary Supplement*, 15 November 1991, n4624: 19.

10. Jean Genet, *Miracle of the Rose*, trans. Bernard Frechtman (New York: Grove Weidenfeld, 1966), 267.

11. Jenkins, 19.

12. Berger, 19.

CHAPTER 6

Queer Views From the Outside: Damned and Damned Proud of It

A number of filmmakers have taken a stab at showing what life is like for those people who don't belong to the mainstream and who, more than that, are having rather a nice time as outcasts. As regards depicting gay life, particularly with an eye trained on those aspects of gay life which the mainstream world finds so horrible, some such filmmakers—most of them openly gay—have presented energetic, independently made films that have had a remarkable success. Perhaps what has made these films so successful is the fact that they have been able to focus on what bugs the world at large about gay people and show it with so much energy and so much confidence that audiences just can't help but enjoy watching. Misery may love company, but even the most bad-tempered sort of person can get caught up in the entertaining vision of people having a good time and being interesting while they do.

The sort of film I'm talking about here is one in which we're invited to look inside the life of someone whom the world would tend, at the very least, to call maladjusted: transvestites, drag queens, sadomasochism enthusiasts, boytoys, those kinds of people. The granddaddy of such films—at least if one considers films that lots of people have seen—is *The Rocky Horror Picture Show* (1975). Based on a highly successful stage play that had a long, successful run in London, this film is one of the most successful cult films of all time, playing continuously at midnight movie theaters for well over a decade. Generally seen as a more or less harmless parody of the Frankenstein story, I find in this raucous romp of a picture several wonderful features that relate to my fascination with homosexuals depicted as monsters. Of course, I'm thinking about Dr. Frank-n-Furter, the part that (I hope) paid Tim Curry's bills for awhile and provided us with one of the most engaging and, if you will pardon me, compelling gay monsters ever to have appeared on the screen. The public loved Tim in this role, and I find reason for a great deal of hope in that fact. I have to confess here that it used to annoy me, when I came out of a late show some years back, to see whole families dressed up like the members of Kiss, waiting politely in line for the umpteenth midnight showing of *Rocky Horror*. Recently I've begun to rethink the issue, and I've finally forgiven all those well-scrubbed suburbanites who stood in line all those nights, clutching their bags of rice. In fact, I more than forgive them; I salute them and bow humbly in the light of the recognition they had when I didn't.

What makes Dr. Frank-n-soforth such a wonderful character is the fact that he isn't simply a parody of the original Doctor. Yes, he is silly and wildly campy, in a way that one imagines, as I do with a sigh, that could not be re-created these days—at least, not as long as Paul and Jan Crouch can find a television camera to stand in front of. I'm thinking here of the scene in which Dr. Frank seduces both Brad and Janet. Isn't he truly scary in that scene? He pops up in both beds like a slip of the tongue and takes his victims in just the way that one might wish, in a very queer mind, that would befall two completely self-unaware people. The success of the film for me centers around how well Tim Curry modulates his performance between shameless camp and the truly frightening power of lawless sexuality. It is frightening to be swept away by desire, and that fact is both funny and terrifying. Who better than a drag queen space alien mad doctor to illustrate the point?

Of course, *Rocky Horror* is a safe view of queer desire presented in all its wickedness. A musical comedy is not meant to be taken as reportage, it's meant to be consumed like a hot fudge sundae. Other films that show queer monsters happily at work tend to be naturally a bit darker, while retaining the edge of fun that helps the pill go down easily. *Priscilla, Queen of the Desert* comes to mind here. Drag queens and a transsexual fed up with their lives embarking on a road trip to play a gig in the Australian outback—there's a nice blend of the ridiculous and the simply, truly touching. "A cock in a frock on a rock"—some came running. Hollywood found this simple little recipe sufficiently appetizing to warrant reconstituting it, virtually verbatim, as a star vehicle in *To Wong Foo, Thanks for Everything, Julie Newmar*. Unfortunately, *To Wong Foo* proved more than anything else that recycling is not always a good thing.

Among underground films, two others stand out for me as depictions of the happily monstrous homosexual: *Pink Narcissus* (1971), by Anonymous, and the much more recent *No Skin Off My Ass*, by Canadian queer director Bruce LaBruce. Odd as it may seem to group these two films together, I think they work as a pair in the way they present a blissful romance between the queerly eroticized male body and the filmmaker. In *Pink Narcissus*, the tropes of porn-pouty-lipped men with huge penises, arranged by physical types and cavorting in a slowly evolving erotic display of the charm of male physicality—are used together with camp elements (jerky, fussy animation and whorehouse decor) to create a backdrop against which we see an archetypal boytoy figure, played by porn star Bobby Kendall, act out the myth of Narcissus. In this queered-up version of the myth, Narcissus turns not into a plant but into an older version of himself from which he recoils in an expression of camp horror. The film seems to take a happy look at the gay male fascination with bodies and big dicks and turn it into an intentionally bathetic burlesque. Of course, one of the principal complaints that mainstream society has levied against homosexuality is its narcissism, and the complaint has always seemed to imply that narcissism is a deadly sin. *Pink Narcissus* seems to be answering that accusation by saying that it isn't so much a sin as a bit of light comedy. Bruce LaBruce's wonderful little film takes the Narcissus story and merges it with Hollywood melodrama (a pastiche of Robert Altman's *That Cold Day in the Park*) and again concludes happily that narcissism is a perfectly respectable pretext for forming a queer relationship.

Pedro Amodovar's wonderful tauromachic spectacle, *La lei del deseo* (*Law of Desire*, 1987), offers another view of fags blissfully living in their own private Idaho and fully possessed by the power of violence in same-sex lust and love. A film in which a man who is driven mad by desire for another man ends his life in gunfire could only be handled in one of two ways, and Almodovar chose wisely to handle it as a visual poem about the irresistibility of passion. True love, the film says, is a disaster, a dark star—that's just the way it is. Who better than a stalker and an artist who has lost control of his life to drive home *that* point?

Then there are John Waters's films, particularly *Desperate Living*, but I would also include *Mondo Trasho*, *Pink Flamingoes* and *Female Trouble* as I consider how much Waters's films are about slaking the thirst of an evidently very wicked public for seeing life lived out by the most excessive creatures found in their exultation. The central figure is, of course, Divine. Nobody believes for a minute that Divine is a woman—only an idiot could believe that he is anything other than an utterly alien creature. Divine is an amalgamation of fearful images, images of some of the most potent transgressions against normalcy our culture can imagine: he is fat, effeminate, he eats poodle shit just for the thrill of it, and he repeatedly impersonates women while making those impersonations transparently awful. He is, after all, a character based on every two-headed calf story, every Liz-abducted-by-space-aliens story that ever appeared in a tabloid. Neither man nor woman, he is the queer image of every bad dream mainstream America ever had about what havoc might be wrought if queerness ever got a good head of steam.

All these films form a group in the way that they depict monstrous characters—lawless misfits, scary oddballs, remorseless criminals—happily living
their lives on the outside of society. Perhaps what makes them most interesting
and most enduring, particularly to gay audiences, is the way they depict a world
in which gay—or queer—characters make a fascinating existence out of the
rubble of life. The characters of these films fascinate us because they aren't interested in fitting in with the world as it's supposed to be. If anything, they
beckon us to join them in a life made of all that has been cast off by mainstream
values. The raw energy they display and the wildness of their worlds present us
with something like Jung's idea of the shadow, the unacknowledged, disowned
self that we fear but that holds the possibility for full creative consciousness.
The central feature of these shadow images is a sense of joy, the joy of embracing the rubble, and from that joy finally issues the power these characters
and worlds have to engage us.

The present work has focused so far on fictional films. While some of
these films employ documentary techniques—such as *My Own Private Idaho*
(with its short documentary codas interspersed among the rest of the scenes),
and *Poison* (with its postmodernist pastiche, in the "Hero" section, of reality
television)—they present themselves preponderantly as fiction. As we survey
the works of lesbian and gay filmmakers to find works that present monstrous
characters, it is interesting to see how variations of the monstrous homosexual
appear in films that employ the trope of documentary film more comprehen-
sively. For example, a filmmaker such as Jennie Livingston, in her film *Paris Is
Burning*, clearly is playing with a queer appropriation of the fashionable notion
of "family values" in building her film around the stories of African American
and Latino drag queens who organize themselves into "houses," surrogate families, in order to survive in a very hostile world. While the Broadway musical
version of *La Cage aux Folles* has enjoyed enormous success (often to predominantly straight audiences), for gay America the mere existence of gay drag
queens has precipitated a rather emotional debate over whether or not drag is a
form of oppressive objectification of women, a gay expression of misogyny.
Thus, for a filmmaker like Livingston (who is a lesbian) to have made a film
that so sympathetically portrays these problematic, transformational monsters
seems clearly to be an instance of a work designed to provoke discomfort about
what "family values" means to the political right as well as to the political left
with which gay activism has tended to identify itself.

Other documentary filmmakers who have played with the notion of monstrosity as it relates to homosexuality are the two German filmmakers Rosa Von
Praunheim and Monika Treut. Beginning in the late 1960s, Von Praunheim began making fictional and nonfictional films (as well as films that employ both
tropes) that presented very disturbing images, particularly of gay men. Some of
these films, such as *It Is Not the Homosexual Who is Perverse, But the Society
in Which He Lives* (released in 1972) presented portrayals of homosexual men
that were so offensive to gay audiences that Von Praunheim has noted that the

greatest criticism he has received has tended to come from gay audiences rather than from straight ones.[1] In *It Is Not the Homosexual Who is Perverse*, von Praunheim presented simpering, weak-willed, stereotypically self-destructive gay men prowling endlessly through public toilets and sleazy bars to feed their insatiable hunger for anonymous sex. When the film was presented for the first time in New York City, audiences vilified the director during a question-and-answer session he attempted to conduct after the film's screening.[2] Later, in 1985, Von Praunheim produced a black musical comedy, *A Virus Knows No Morals*, in which he himself appeared as a monstrously unscrupulous gay bathhouse owner who, when he himself is stricken by AIDS, turns into an even more unsympathetic character: a whining mama's boy who continually keeps asking, Why me? Recently, in 1992, Von Praunheim raised a few eyebrows by presenting his docudrama, *Ich Bin Meine Eigene Frau* (*I Am My Own Woman*), which chronicles the life of Charlotte Von Mahlsdorf, the extraordinary gay man who has lived in drag since adolescence and who, for his lifelong efforts at historical preservation of architecture and furniture, recently became the first transvestite to receive the German government's highest civilian honor, the Cross of the Order of Merit. In this film, Von Praunheim invites gay and straight audiences not merely to look sympathetically at an "objectionable" gay character but also to witness the events through which that character comes to be recognized as a national hero.

Ich bin meine eigene Frau is a documentary film that focuses on showing deviance as a positive, creative state of being. The film, documents the life of the remarkable: Charlotte Von Mahlsdorf, born Lothar Berfelde. At the end of Von Praunheim's film, we see Lottchen (as friends call Lothar/Charlotte, with genuine affection), dressed in a tastefully simple white blouse and simple black skirt, his shoulder-length, white hair arranged in a flattering pageboy style about his handsome face (unadorned with makeup, which has always been Lottchen's style), accepting the Cross of the Order of Merit from the German Minister of Culture. Lottchen, standing proudly as the Minister pins the Cross to his blouse, curtsies neatly and looks out into an audience of popping flashbulbs. The smile on his face shows a difficult if full life vindicated. He has withstood the brutality of the National Socialists under Hitler, the Stasi (state secret police) under the Deutsche Demokratische Republik, and the disenfranchised right-wing radicals of post-German reunification, and now (s)he stands before the German nation, a happy, old, very "out" homosexual man wearing a dress, being regaled as a national hero.

Documenting the vindication of admittedly eccentric, happily perverse gay life is, from beginning to end, the central concern of this film.[3] The film, which takes its title from Von Mahlsdorf's recently published autobiography (*Ich Bin Meine Eigene Frau*), employs a formally perverse method to present what Jean Cocteau might have called "a lie which tells the truth": an artful mixture of fictional and factual elements—first-person accounts, informal conversations, dramatic reenactments and commentaries on those reenactments—aimed at ren-

dering the truest possible representation of Lottchen's life. What this representation gives us is the portrait of a person who fully embraces and exploits that
within his own character which mainstream culture tends to regard as monstrous—being an openly, proudly effeminate homosexual transvestite—and who
builds a long, fulfilling life around that character.

Behind Lottchen is the filmmaker himself. Like his subject, Von Praunheim
changed his name to that of a woman early in his career as an artist.[4] Inserting
the word *von* into their new names, both men indulged, early in their careers, in
a queer joke: *von* functions in German names as a tag indicating that the name's
bearer is a member of the nobility. As part of the process of their rituals of
queer self-naming, both men have publicly tagged themselves as being *queens*.
This gesture, assuming the label of a female persona, marks both Rosa and Lottchen as being pioneers in appropriating the tag "queer" as part of coming out.
Given this link between the two men's names, we are invited by the film to read
Lottchen's story as clearly relating to Von Praunheim's own life.

Starting out in the 1960s as a painter, Rosa (who was born almost a generation after Lottchen) soon moved to filmmaking, and by the late sixties was already making short documentary and feature films aimed at addressing emerg-
ing lesbian and gay communities. From the very beginning, Rosa exhibited a
strong sense of dialectic in his filmmaking: his films tend to be based on a peda-
gogical method of opposition by means of which he often presents unsettling
aspects of gay character aimed at producing a serious dialogue within his audience. Through the dialogue his films create, Rosa clearly intends lesbians and
gay men to take a serious critical look at themselves as individuals and as members of a community. The critical look Rosa promotes is concerned with making
(primarily) gay men examine how their behavior and attitudes about themselves
contribute to their own oppression. This character of Rosa's films has thus often
put him at odds with the gay community, especially in the United States. For
instance, as mentioned above, when in 1972 Rosa attended the first screening in
New York of his film *It Is Not the Homosexual Who Is Perverse, But the Society
in Which He Lives*, he was harshly criticized by the largely gay audience, who
were incensed at the film's "negative" portraits of gay men. The film depicted
stereotypically fey gay characters who use each other for sex and who are unable to defend themselves from the ill-treatment leveled against them by straight
people. Many people in the audience felt that Rosa was simply using the film to
reinforce stereotypes of the homosexual as an inherently weak and sick character type.

Rosa responded then, and continues to respond to this criticism, by saying
that what he sought to do with this film was expose the fact that gay people participate in their own oppression by refusing to acknowledge a few important
truths about themselves: that most gay people live in the closet and compensate
for doing so by leading clandestine lives, and that such lives tend to be centered
around compartmentalizing one's being gay within the confines of anonymous
sex; that by supporting this way of living, they deny each other publicly and

help to maintain the notion that homosexuality is a secret that needs to be guarded; and, perhaps most importantly, that the character of gay men often deviates significantly from that of most heterosexual men—many gay men are effeminate, and many gay men structure their relationships and their manner of living in ways that mainstream society labels as unmanly—and that this deviance needs to be acknowledged and talked about openly, not denied by people who would like us to say that there is no difference between gay men and straight men. In effect, Von Praunheim seems to be saying with this film that the notion that homosexuality is monstrous—a shameful social ill—derives largely from what gay people do to themselves and to each other, and not merely from what the straight world does to them.[5]

Rosa maintains that by exposing that which the gay community does not like to see or say about itself, he is simply concerned with making change: if we do not openly talk about what is uncomfortable to us, we cannot change it. If we deny ourselves, we cannot band together. And if we do not talk openly about ourselves, we cannot claim the power it takes for us to survive. In other words, as long as gay people refuse to talk about the unpleasant aspects of being gay, we help to maintain our status as victims.

Another of Rosa's early films, *Army of Lovers, or Revolt of the Perverts* uses another angle to employ the strategy of exposing heretofore unmentionable aspects of gay life as a way of divesting those aspects of their power to shock people. In this film the director records his having sex with a male porn star. Part of what makes the filming particularly provocative is the fact that Von Praunheim produced the film with the assistance of students from the filmmaking class he was teaching at San Francisco State College. Having intentionally failed to tell his students beforehand what the subject of the filming would be, Rosa directed his students to film him as his partner and he caressed, undressed each other, and performed oral sex. He also directed the students to film each other as they reacted to what his partner and he were doing, so that the film records a number of very interesting facial expressions among the film crew. What appears most evident in these facial expressions is not disgust or anger, but anxiety, so that the film takes the form of a visual point-counterpoint in which we see the film crew's anxiety on the one hand and the performing couple's surprisingly unselfconscious pleasure on the other. In commenting about his intention for the film, Rosa has noted that what he wanted to do was to expose exactly those aspects of being gay that most people do not want to look at, hoping that by doing so, he would rid the forbidden images of gay sex of their shock value.[6] Clearly, in doing this, Rosa seems to be addressing centrally the straight world's notion that to be gay is to be a monster of a certain, very powerful type: a species of monster so powerful that we cannot bear to look at it. By forcing his audience to look at the most threateningly monstrous images of gayness, he is taking steps to bring the monster into the light, revealing it to be nothing very extraordinary at all, but rather being just another variety of normalcy—desire expressing itself.

All of this brings us back to *I Am My Own Woman*: if vindicating Lottchen and Rosa is a central intention of the film, an important part of that vindication consists in showing the bravery and idealism in what the straight world tends to call deviant in homosexual men.[7] Lottchen is clearly depicted in the film as a perfect lady: her (and from here on, that is the pronoun we will use for Lottchen) diction is textbook perfect (very unusual for a person who has spent her life in and around Berlin, with its distinctive accent), her manner of speaking impeccably ladylike without being ridiculous. Lottchen is not a drag queen, but rather a transvestite, as she says repeatedly throughout the film. She dresses simply and tastefully, wearing no makeup and always dressing in the neatly simple manner of a German housewife. At several points in the film, Lottchen tells us that the model for her feminine character was her own mother, telling us at one point that she is the "spitting image" of her mother. From what we know of the lady—Lottchen's reminiscences of her—she was a lovely, good, simple, gentle, long-suffering woman who loved her son. Feeling the close connection with her mother and identifying with her so completely, Lottchen explains further that she is a "weibliches Wesen im männlichem Körper" (literally, "a feminine being in a masculine body") indicating the influence of her early readings of the work of Magnus Hirschfeld, the German sexologist who sought to normalize the phenomenon of homosexuality by explaining it as a third sex, intermediate between the male and female sexes. Estranged from her brutal father, who was a committed Nazi, Lottchen found sympathy as a teenager in her aunt Luise, whom she visited regularly. This lady, Lottchen discovered, was a lesbian who also lived as a transvestite, living in men's clothing on her private estate and surrounding herself with carefully selected people who were sympathetic to her manner of living. Discovering a kindred spirit in the young Lothar (Lottchen), Aunt Luise gave the young boy girls' clothes, books by Hirschfeld, unflagging tolerance and encouragement, and a strapping stableboy to play with. In this idyllic setting, Lottchen was able to develop happily along the inclinations of her own nature, growing into a quiet sense of her own normalcy as a homosexual transvestite as she developed an interest in womanly things— playing with dolls, cleaning house, and tending to furniture—which activities became the primary occupations of her adult life. Devoted to her mother, who was brutalized by her Nazi father, Lottchen was obliged towards the end of the World War II to kill her father by beating him to death when the latter threatened to kill her mother and siblings. Sentenced for this crime to a youth reformatory, Lottchen lived out the rest of the war as a fugitive when, having been released by officials from the reformatory during the chaos of Germany in early 1945, she set out on her own to survive.

From the point she was released from the reformatory, Lottchen began a life as, in her own words, *her own woman*, which life she continued to live up until and including the time of the making of Rosa's film. Released into the *Trümmerwelt* of postwar Germany, Lottchen was able to begin living as a transvestite. In the disorder of post-World War II Germany, she found herself, as a matter of political accident, in the zone administered by the Russians, which ultimately became East Germany. From the end of the war until the mid-sixties, however, it does not appear that Lottchen was significantly affected, for the most part, by the presence of the new political order. Taking up residence in an abandoned palace, Lottchen did something remarkable: she cleaned, scrubbed, rebuilt and refurnished the palace on her own, with no help and virtually no income. In taking up this activity, she was able to realize the principal fantasy of her adolescence: to live a quiet life as a German housewife, caring for her home. As part of realizing this fantasy, Lottchen assembled from the rubble around her a vast collection of discarded antique furniture and other household effects.

When the East German government became aware of her accomplishment, they sought to seize the house and the furnishings that Lottchen had so painstakingly rebuilt and restored. Unable to resist the government, Lottchen moved out of the house and gave away most of the furnishings she had collected and placed in the huge palace. Finding another abandoned house—a large, late-nineteenth-century manor house outside Berlin in a suburb called Mahlsdorf (hence the name Charlotte *von Mahlsdorf*)—Lottchen again took up residence in a ruin, again restored it and furnished it, eventually opened it to the public as a museum, and was again pursued by the East German government, who tried unsuccessfully to seize her second collection of treasures.

Lottchen's collection consisted of artifacts from the period that fascinated her the most: the German *Gründerzeit*, the period of late-Victorian German culture from roughly 1880 until 1900. At one point in the film, Lottchen explains to us that what most endeared this period and its artifacts to her was the fact that her great uncle, one of her two favorite people, had lived in a house built and furnished in the manner of this period. Resisting the government of what she repeatedly calls in the film the *Verbrecherstaat* (criminal state), Lottchen again gave away most of her collection of artifacts and managed to hold on to the house by conducting guided tours for a fee.

Very soon (the film is vague on dates, but we can infer from what Lottchen tells us that she took up residence in the manor house in Mahlsdorf sometime in the early 1960s) the house became a center of gay culture in East Germany, and again Lottchen calmly, cleverly resisted the attempts by the Stasi in the early 1970s to use her as an informant to implicate the gay men and lesbians who gathered in her house (as a house rule, visitors were known by first name only). While providing a safe house for gay men and lesbians, Lottchen also formally learned furniture restoration by working at the Märkische Museum in Berlin, and she established a close working relationship with the East German film industry, first by loaning furnishings and antique clothing and later by acting in films herself (usually in the role of an elderly female aunt in period dramas). After the Berlin Wall came down in 1991 (significantly, Lottchen tells us, on the same day as the premiere of East Germany's first major gay commercial film, *Coming Out*, in which Lottchen played a role as a transvestite barkeeper), Lottchen continued to gather gay men and lesbians around her at her home in

Mahlsdorf, where she organized the first, post-reunification gay and lesbian festival. This festival proved to be the occasion of a highly publicized riot in which skinheads attacked the assembly of five hundred people, breaking into the house, vandalizing the premises and brutally beating a great many people. Commenting on the aftermath of the violence, Lottchen calmly notes that she has withstood the violence of the Nazis and the Stasi, and that she is determined to keep living as she always has.

As Lottchen tells the remarkable story of her survival, she also tells us along the way the story of her love life. Beginning with the period after the end of the Second World War, Lottchen cultivates a singularly fulfilling series of romantic attachments, one of them lasting approximately twenty-five years, with men who share her fascination with transvestitism, bondage and discipline, and elaborate sexual role-playing. The sections of the film that portray these rela-tionships, most of them presented as docudramatic reenactments, stress the tenderness and happiness that Lottchen has found throughout her life in sexual attachments with other men that mainstream society wound tend to find de-praved and disease-ridden. In Lottchen's recollection of this aspect of her life, however, what is emphasized clearly is the satisfaction and mutual caring that deviance has brought her.[8]

To support the sense of normalcy in Lottchen's sense of her sexual identity, Rosa inserts a number of scenes in the film that reenact Lottchen's sexual en-counters at various stages in her life. Employing reenactments also to depict other important points in Lottchen's life—being beaten by her father, escaping the Allied bombing of Berlin at the end of World War II—Rosa employs such scenes primarily to give the viewer of the film a lightly humorous, close and personal look at Lottchen's sex life. All of these scenes are quite daring in that they deal with subjects that, even among gay audiences, would be considered taboo or problematic. For instance, in one such scene, we see the actor who portrays Lottchen as a teenager, aged somewhere between fifteen and seven-teen, having sex with Aunt Luise's stableboy, an obviously older man. The ac-tor portraying Lottchen at this point, an angelically beautiful young man named Jens Taschner, looks young enough to be a NAMBLA (National Association of Man-Boy Love) poster child. When we see him cavorting in the nude with his older partner in a hayloft (no explicit sexual act is shown, only caressing and kissing), we must recognize that we are dangerously close to pornography. The film obliges us to ask a serious question here: Is Rosa, by depicting a young boy in a sexual situation with an older man, feeding into the straight world's view of homosexuals as being essentially sick, predatory abusers of children? Is it an indication of some sort of essential sickness for an audience to allow itself to look with fascination and pleasure at a young man, possibly still a boy, being sexual with a grown man? The film answers these question for us by bringing another viewer into the scene. This viewer is Aunt Luise, who enters the scene (the interior of the barn on her estate) looking for her stableboy. At first vexed because she finds that the stableboy has left his work in the barn, Aunt Luise climbs into the hayloft and, discovering her nephew and servant *in flagrante delicto*, excuses herself sweetly, apologizing for interrupting and telling them, as she departs, to take their time. Structuring the scene in these ways—depicting the sex between young Lothar/Lottchen and an adult man "tastefully," as a scene of sweet caresses, and legitimating the sex through Aunt Luise's *avuncular* blessing—serves very well in the film to deflate any sense that the scene is depicting anything wrong or wrongly.

In another reenactment scene, we see Lottchen (portrayed at this point by Ichgola Androgyn, whose appearance and demeanor perfectly match his name) as a young twenty-something, established in a *menage* with an older man, a German aristocrat several decades older than she. The arrangement between the two people is clearly depicted as being based on fetishes played as a form of *heimliche Zärtlichkeit* (homespun tenderness): Lottchen cleans the elder man's house, dressed in short shorts, blouse and Carmen Miranda clogs, providing the older gentleman with considerable pleasure as she bends over to do her dusting and cleaning. The elder man, clearly appreciating Lottchen's allure, gently (but masterfully) grabs her and places her on his lap, and confesses his attraction. The scene then cuts to show Lottchen and the elder man posing before an antique camera (originating, no doubt, from Lottchen's beloved *Gründerzeit*, with the elderly gentleman sitting in for Lottchen's favorite uncle in a living realization of a youthful fantasy). The poses depict various bondage and discipline tableaux, with Lottchen blissfully being spanked by the proudly smiling aristocrat. The visual manner in which these scenes is presented succeeds well in conveying not depravity but wholesomeness: the actors reenacting these events indicate, through sincere and delicate gestures rather than words, a sense of politely refined pleasure that the two men exchange among themselves.

It seems that what Von Praunheim is doing most completely in this film is confront us as viewers with two incompatible propositions between which we must choose. One proposition allows us to judge all that we see of Lottchen as being straightforward evidence of the sickness of homosexuality: she is preoccupied with sex in general and with fetishes in particular, and she is the image of gender confusion. The other proposition allows us to see in her deviance the source of her personal strength and success: she decided early on in life what and who she wanted to be, she became that person, and she achieved happiness as a result of doing so.

To appreciate fully how much the film is structured around showing Lottchen's life as a success, it is important to note how little the film focuses on the difficulties Lottchen experienced in living as she chose to live. Murdering her father and escaping from the Nazis are depicted in the film as significant events, but as being minor in their effect on Lottchen's character in comparison to the effect of being surrounded for most of her life by people who loved her. When the film shows Lottchen dealing with the Stasi or with the homophobes of East (or West) Germany, it shows her summarily dismissing them with ladylike aplomb and grace. However, the scenes that deal with the truly difficult side of

what, perhaps, should have been a very difficult life, amount to relatively little
in the film as a whole. Most of what we see of Lottchen in the film is a person
whose life has been built around the certainty of who she is and who has found,
by virtue of the careful, loving attention she has given to being herself and being with other people, a great measure of happiness.

Perhaps the scene in the film that most clearly sums up this certainty and its
triumphant effects is the one in which Lottchen is called into the office of a
Communist Party official at the Märkische Museum in Berlin, where, during the
1960s, Lottchen was employed as an apprentice in antique furniture restoration.
Confronted by the official with the rumor that he (Lothar) had been seen the
evening before at a party wearing women's clothes, Lottchen was asked by the
official to reassure him that the rumor was false. "On the contrary," replied
Lottchen (here portrayed by Lottchen herself) "I was wearing a yellow cocktail
dress, a pearl necklace, and a lovely blonde wig." Understanding that by making
this confession, she is positioning herself to be dismissed from her work at the
museum, Lottchen concludes the conversation by telling the incredulous appa-
ratchik, "It makes absolutely no difference whether I go about town wearing a
dress or whatever I please." This is what it means for Lottchen to say *I am my
own woman*: it means that she understands who she is, and that no matter how
much who she is differs from what is expected of her, she will not consent to
change herself to meet those expectations.

Monika Treut's feature films, such as *Virgin Machine* and *Seduction: the
Cruel Woman*, have tended to focus on what mainstream society would tend to
view as being dark figures: transsexuals and lesbian or bisexual dominatrixes
who rule serenely over harems of sex slaves. In Treut's hands these characters
are blissfully well adjusted to the darkness of their lives. In her portrayals of
such characters, Treut focuses on showing deviance as a means by which some
people make a fundamental choice about how to structure their private lives. By
making these choices about how to live, Treut implies, these people are living
constructively by taking control of their lives; as such, they stand as models of
personal freedom.[9] Essentially, Treut's films view the world from the stand-
points of varying types of social monster (most of them women), presenting her
characters' monstrous values as being matter-of-factly natural.

Treut's film *Female Misbehavior*, released in 1992, is a documentary film
that presents monstrous women—some lesbian, others defying sexual categori-
zation—in such a way as to take as natural what the world at large would tend
to see as their deviance. Actually a compendium of four films produced by
Treut between 1982 and 1992, these four short films, titled *Dr. Paglia*, *Annie
Sprinkle*, *Bondage*, and *Max*, present four characters who find power, not problems, in their own deviance. Two of the films, *Bondage* and *Annie Sprinkle*,
were exhibited by Treut at film festivals for several years before she assembled
them with the other two films to make *Female Misbehavior*.[10] Like her feature
films, the four short films that comprise *Female Misbehavior* concern them-

selves with portrayals of sexual deviance in women in such a way as to emphasize its ordinariness.[11]

The four films that make up *Female Misbehavior* move in a peripatetic way
through a presentation of the ordinariness of female deviance in different forms.
Dr. Paglia presents Camille Paglia as a fast-talking, entertainingly clownlike (if
not ridiculously self-promoting) self-styled academic Amazon on a mission: to
have all the sex she wants and to reform what she repeatedly refers to as the
current phase of victim-oriented, politically correct but culturally ignorant, spu-
rious feminism. *Annie Sprinkle* presents the now infamous porno star turned
performance artist as she performs her art: transforming herself from the rather
dowdy Ellen Steinberg to the blissfully happy sex goddess Annie Sprinkle,
dressed in a wardrobe out of the Frederick's of Hollywood catalogue, complete
with alarmingly high heels; using her massive, exposed breasts to provide choreographed accompaniment to music and to adorn the heads of audience members during her cabaret act; and, as part of the same cabaret performance, inserting a speculum into her vagina and inviting the audience to examine her
cervix with a flashlight. *Bondage* presents a woman, unidentified in the film,
who is an aficionada of leather and bondage, as she discusses with almost clini-
cal sincerity the elaborate rituals she practices by herself and with her sex partners. In addition to discussing these matters, the film's one character holds forth
at length on the mission she feels is her position of stewardship as an enlightened bondage enthusiast: to address groups of women (including one in Maine)
on the potential for empowerment and self-discovery that bondage holds for
women. And the final film in the set, *Max*, presents a Native American who is in
the early stages of undergoing a female-to-male sex change. Max is presented as
a calmly resolved person who has found his true path: having lived through a
stage of traditional, heterosexual womanhood followed by a period of lesbian
attachments, Max has finally learned that he is not a lesbian, but rather a heterosexual man in a woman's body. Throughout these four films, Treut presents
highly personal portraits of her characters that focus on some aspect of deviance
that those characters take as centrally defining their lives, as defining normalcy
at a personal level. Taken as a whole, these four portraits form a more or less
unified image of female deviance secure in its own validity.

One striking feature that runs throughout the four films is the way that
Treut allows her subjects, for the most part, simply to speak for themselves. In
the case of Dr. Paglia, there may have been no other alternative to this approach. In one dizzying diatribe, Paglia describes, *molto allegro, con vivace*, an
early stage of her sentimental education. As a child in the 1950s, Paglia tells us,
she felt alienated from Christianity's "turn the other cheek" ethos (which, she
reports, no Italian really ever believed in) and felt intuitively drawn at an early
age to the monumentality of ancient Egyptian culture as evidenced in the giant,
engraved steles she viewed in museums. In the imposing icons she saw on these
sculptures, Paglia notes, she perceived a connection with advertisements on the
backs of the cereal boxes she used to pore over at the family breakfast table.

Too young to read, she was only able to ponder the inscrutability of cereal box icons; thus the inscrutable runes and bas-reliefs of ancient sculpture held for her a fascination that tied them in purpose to cereal box ads: the Egyptians were advertising themselves, she notes, and what has survived for us of the message of these ancient advertisements is the sheer phallic monumentality with which ancient Egyptian culture invested itself.

By allowing Paglia to present this discourse with virtually no interruption from the interviewer (who is Treut herself in this scene, occasionally seen in the corner of the frame of the camera, ceaselessly nodding but never asking a question or offering a comment), Treut allows her subject to enlarge herself to fill the whole screen through the content of her speech—with its perplexing logical movement—and the manner of her performance. The character of this enlargement is one of a sort of dynamic monstrosity: Paglia is allowed simultaneously to act out, on the one hand, her own monumental sense of self importance and brilliance and, on the other, her outrageously clownlike, comically diminished character.

In much of the rest of the film, Paglia discusses with an unnamed male companion her unique position as a "bisexual lesbian": because she is such a powerful woman *and* because she is so laughable, she explains in a *pizzicato* speech, she frightens prospective female sex partners away; because she tires quickly of male lovers once, as she says, they break the law of seduction by falling in love, she is doomed to live without sexual satisfaction. Whether she is holding forth on her identification with Egyptian statuary or on her puzzlement over the sexual isolation that results from the force of her character, Paglia presents herself (or is allowed by Treut to present herself) as a singularly enlarged character by nature. Thus enlarged, Paglia becomes monstrous in the film by virtue of her implied size: deliriously happy with her own position as a misfit— with respect to her academic colleagues, with respect to the majority of feminists, and with respect to other lesbians—she continually asserts her being monumentally off-center as the source of her strength and of the validity of her way of life.

Another device Treut uses to enlarge Paglia's presence in the film is to employ an unnamed interviewer in the film who is apparently an initiate in Paglia's world. This person, who is obviously a male friend of Paglia's, speaks at some length with Paglia about her sex life. As he obviously knows Paglia quite well, he is able to give the impression of speaking informally as he asks Paglia (or mostly, as he listens to her talk) about her unique position as a woman who is a powerful intellectual and whose sexual life is colored by the character of her greatness. If Treut herself had taken the position of the interviewer in these scenes, the conversations might have had a more adversarial tone. A more formal interviewing partner might certainly have asked Paglia whether she expects to be taken seriously. The male interviewer of the film, however, never asks such a question. Rather than questioning Paglia's sense of her own monumentality, he asks her to describe it and to analyze it, thus reinforcing the sense that it is a *given* that Paglia is, in fact, as extraordinary as she claims she is.

Just as she employs several devices to create the impression that Paglia is being allowed to tell her own truth, to document herself faithfully, Treut also interjects herself into the film as a critical presence that questions and, perhaps, undermines Paglia's statements about herself. Treut does this by inserting, at several points in the film, footage from old documentary films. In one such instance, after hearing from Paglia that part of her mission in life is to shake up the status quo of victim-based feminism, we see silent film footage (obviously shot during the late 1920s or early 1930s) of obese women being comically throttled, massaged and shaken by machines in a health spa. The comic visual character of the old film footage clearly is meant to be seen as a comment on the comical nature of Paglia's own discourse. Always speaking in the film in a tempo reminiscent of Gilbert and Sullivan (the aria "I Am the Very Model of a Modern Major General" from *The Pirates of Penzance* comes especially to mind here), Paglia invariably slices, dices and tosses her points of argument into an improbable mixture. In her discourse on what is wrong with feminism, to give another example, Paglia lays out her own version of a true feminist credo: she is for war, for snuff films (provided they do not involve actually killing people), for pornography in general, and she is against "neopuritanism" (by which she appears to mean the tendency among some feminists to find men culpable and women essentially vulnerable in most sexual transactions) or anything else that attempts to circumscribe the limits of acceptable human behavior, especially in the realm of art. In the manner of her delivery, Paglia makes it evident that she takes it as obvious that her credo fairly well covers all the major issues that a truly exhaustive credo should. The very force of her delivery makes it evident that Paglia is challenging us to validate what she says not so much by virtue of the logical rigor of her discourse as by virtue of her passionate insistence that her credo is self-evidently true.

By choosing to intervene critically into Paglia's self-presentation as she does (with the old movie footage), Treut is certainly giving the viewer the room to see Paglia simply as a fool. But this is not to say that the film itself clearly leaves us with a comfortable conviction that foolishness is all there is to Dr. Paglia. Paglia herself observes often in the film (especially when accounting for her dismal track record with female sex partners) that she is a laughable person. Having made this pronouncement about herself, Paglia simply adds being laughable to the list of characteristics that mark her very special character. If, as she so often asserts, it is her intention to be a gadfly buzzing about the "establishment," Paglia's self-admitted silliness may be understood as a supremely *queer* performance of dandyism: like Wilde, Paglia never seems to speak seriously about serious matters; like Wilde, her vehemence is a mockery of sincerity. In the end, Paglia herself (naturally) has the last word: as the film concludes, she turns to the camera and addresses her enemies among the intelligentsia, telling them to "eat my dust."

The second film in the series, *Annie Sprinkle*, appears to be the most purely documentary section of *Female Misbehavior*. In this short film, the subject is allowed to present herself with no readily apparent critical intervention by Treut. As Sprinkle is a performance artist, this approach makes a great deal of sense. What we see of Annie Sprinkle is her performance itself, acted out and presented in still photographs. The film thus frames the viewer's field of comprehension within the framework of an audience viewing Sprinkle's act. As the film begins, we see a still photograph of a woman as we hear voice-over narration that explains what we are seeing. What we see is an image of a woman, an unflattering, black-and-white image of Ellen Steinberg. Ellen is an ordinary-looking woman who, the female voice-over narrator tells us, becomes transformed into the alter-ego Annie Sprinkle through the application of makeup and provocative clothing. As the narrator completes her explanation of this transformation, we see the transformation itself take place in moving pictures shot in color: the static, black-and-white Ellen Steinberg thus becomes the dynamic, colorful Annie Sprinkle. Annie, we now learn, is the narrator of the film, speaking for herself and for Ellen. The visual logic of the film thus establishes the notion that Annie is more real than Ellen. Annie is animated and happy, while Ellen is dull and dispirited; Annie moves all the time, Ellen cannot move at all; and Annie speaks, while Ellen does not. Here Treut again frames the presentation of her subject so as to take it as a given that a sort of female deviance—a woman's valorizing her highly fetishistic alter ego over her unadorned self—is self-evidently natural.

Having allowed her subject to present the naturalness of her transformation, Treut then follows Sprinkle as she performs. The instrument of this performance is Annie Sprinkle's body itself.[12] Dressed in seductive boudoir clothes accentuated by long, lacquered fingernails and five-inch heels, Annie displays her breasts, her buttocks and her genitals while she explains how she uses her body in her performance. What stands out most about her explanation is its manner: as she explains how, having large breasts, she exposes them and places them onto the heads of audience members during her cabaret act so that they can have souvenir pictures made, Sprinkle sounds as if she is explaining how to make chicken divan or how to do the cross-stitch. When, seated on stage, she inserts a speculum into her vagina and then allows the camera to view her cervix with the aid of a flashlight (which process we see also in still shots taken from her actual cabaret act), Sprinkle presents herself with a casual delight suggesting that you (the audience) can also do this at home.

Sprinkle's presentation of herself (or Treut's presentation of her presentation) employs a form of monstrosity to overturn the fetishizing heterosexual male gaze. By monstrosity here I mean that Sprinkle, like Paglia, is presented in the film as being a monumentally enlarged image that takes pleasure in itself. As we watch Sprinkle in the film, we are led to feel that her performance is not at all about the pleasure of being looked at; her performance is, rather, about the pleasure of exhibiting oneself. More specifically, Sprinkle's exhibition of herself consists of a series of acts by which she pulls her audience into a close-up view of her eroticized body so as to allow the audience to *see* her pleasure in herself in as large a form as she herself experiences it. Her body thus becomes a monumentally enlarged image that exposes the transgressive nature of desire. Focusing on men's fascination with looking at vaginas, Sprinkle takes her audience *inside* her own vagina, announcing clearly as she does so that she takes pleasure in her own body's beauty. The point of exposing her cervix is to set up what first looks like the "normal" act of looking with fascination at an eroticized object, and then to invite her audience to take a much closer look than it would ordinarily allow itself to take. The close-up view she offers of herself then shatters this fascination by exaggerating its mechanics and thus transforms the act of looking from one in which the objectifying gaze takes its pleasure to one in which the objectifier is forced to see the objectified's taking pleasure in itself. In effect, Sprinkle is deflating the notion of transgression by taking something naughty—being fascinated with vaginas—too far, not for the sake of the looker, but for her own pleasure irrespective of her audience.

The pleasure of exhibitionism also plays an important role in the third short film, entitled *Bondage*. In this film, an unnamed woman stands before the camera and talks about her interest in bondage and sadomasochism and her self-defined mission of making women more aware of their sexuality. Heavy set and rather menacing looking, this woman speaks calmly into the camera as she describes and demonstrates such acts as nipple torture (at one point she uses the alligator clip attached to her microphone as an erotic device); placing her sex partner (or being placed herself) into an elaborate sling she has set up in her apartment; and designing and wearing in public her own special bondage attire. What the speaker emphasizes as she describes these activities is that they are all designed both to increase awareness of one's body and, more importantly, to create a feeling of being safe and protected. As the speaker argues it, bondage is not about hurting people; it is about using pain to make one more aware of one's body's potential for erotic feeling, and it is about using devices of containment to enable a person (the speaker is clearly interested only in women—she clearly points out that her philosophy does not concern itself with the experience of men) to feel safe and free. For instance, when she describes the routines surrounding being suspended in a sling, the speaker emphasizes that a suspended person has a feeling of floating freely. When she describes the attention she pays to putting a person in bondage, the speaker emphasizes the care she takes to attending to the comfort of her partner. What makes these routines work successfully towards promoting pleasure, the speaker says repeatedly, is the clarity with which the participants communicate with one another to use the devices of bondage to enable a feeling of emotional comfort and delight.

As she makes her case, the speaker presents herself sincerely as being concerned with promoting the betterment of women. For her, focusing on women's feeling pleasure and on attaining a feeling of safety is a serious life mission. In her presentation, she takes it for granted that bondage and sadomasochism are constructive, affirmative means of attaining these ends. As she talks, she never takes a defensive posture towards fetishism: she never brings into her discourse an apology for deviance. By excluding such a defense from her presentation and by arguing so consistently for the benefits that fetishism offers, she clearly overturns the notion that deviance means sickness by promoting deviant desire as a means towards achieving personal health.

In the fourth film of the series, *Max*, Treut sets up the narrative of the film so as to surprise us. As the film begins, we see a very masculine-looking person, obviously Asian or Native American, as he begins to tell his story. It is only after he has spoken for a few minutes that we learn that this person is, in fact, a biological female: having begun to undergo a series of hormone treatments as part of a sex change, the person to whom we have been introduced is actually a woman who wants to become a man.

The film tends to focus on allowing us to see and hear this person, Max, as he tells his story. Only after the film has visually established for us that this person is *clearly* a man—he has a deep voice, unaffected, "naturally" masculine mannerisms (frequently throughout the film, we see him shadow-boxing, strutting very convincingly, or sitting in a manly pose)—does it allow us to see the "before" pictures: still shots of an attractive young woman becoming more and more radically stylized in her look, starting out with long, feminine hair and good skin and ending with a multicolored, spiked coiffure accentuated by heavily applied makeup. The still shots then serve to give us a context for Max's transformation: the several stages of "his" femininity are presented as static shots, a history of what was, as prologue to the totally changed presence we see before us: a real man.

As Max tells his story, he does so with the calm assumption that his is a rather unexceptional story. He started out as a regular girl, became a lesbian, finally figured out that he was a heterosexual man in a woman's body, and that was that. Most of what Max tells us centers around describing matter-of-factly how he goes about his life at this stage: having undergone hormone treatments, he now feels like a man, pumped full of testosterone and feeling good and sexy. He still has a woman's breasts, which he tapes to his body to conceal, and he wears what he calls, in the lingo of female-to-male sex changes, a "stuffer"—a soft plastic rat (significantly enough) he bought in a novelty store, which he has placed in a piece of pantyhose and then stuffed into his trousers to create the appearance of his having a penis. As he discusses his penis, Max walks us through the options open to him for having various types of operation designed to produce an organic prosthesis which will function as a "real" penis. One such procedure involves having a nerve and muscle tissue transplant from his arm to grow an artificial penis and attach it onto his own pudenda. The other process involves surgery to alter "his" clitoris so as to enlarge it and shape it into a penis-like process. Neither procedure produces perfect results, but Max shrugs off the inconvenience as part of the package he has to deal with. The essence of what he says about his transformation and how he says it is that he is certain about it: he knows he is a man, and he is determined to get what he wants.

Including *Max* in *Female Misbehavior* may seem, at first glance, to involve a fundamental contradiction. If, on the one hand, we look at the other three short films in this collection, it is not too difficult for us to gather from them a more or less coherent sense of theme: depicting women leading happy lives strongly focused on sexual deviance. If we look at the character Max, on the other hand, it appears we have a character who is profoundly wounded by misogyny, a woman so taken in by Western culture's devaluation of womanhood that she has decided to become a he.[13] Though this reading of Max is certainly possible, I believe it is equally possible to see Max as complementing the other characters in *Female Misbehavior* in a few very important senses. If, for example, we take Max at face value just as Treut presents him, we have to believe that, however it may be true, he has reached a position of comfort with his sexual identity as it has developed during his transformation.

Whatever else we may think of Max, we cannot deny, having listened to him in the film, that he views his own sexuality positively. That is, the discovery that he is a male identity living in a female body represents, to Max, an advance in his awareness, an advance which has brought him personal contentment. Stating clearly in the film that he can never make a complete transition from having a female body to having a truly male one, Max argues in the film that it is his knowledge of his identity that is the source of his contentment. In saying this, he implicitly admits that he has embraced being a deviant, saying, at one point, that his choice to transform himself is not about trying to "fit in" with mainstream society in some way. By accepting his own deviance, then, Max has come to construct a personal identity that affirms his freedom to choose who he is. Exercising the freedom to choose one's identity then clearly links Max with Annie Sprinkle, the persona who replaces Ellen Steinberg as a matter of choice. Similarly, freedom to choose links Max with the central character of *Bondage*, who repeatedly tells us that the sexual routines of bondage she practices are meant to create a sense of freedom. And finally, freedom to choose comes through in much of what Paglia says, as she asserts her right not to be told by feminists that women are victims, and as she refuses to live her life as if she, herself, were a victim.

In the last analysis, *Female Misbehavior* remains true to its subject by refusing to offer its political statement to any particular camp.[14] Paglia's attacks on feminism, Sprinkle's exploitation of pornography, the dominatrix's affirmation of the value of bondage, and Max's celebration of gender reassignment do not add up to a political position that any version of feminism could easily appropriate. By making the film finally so problematic, Treut herself has committed an act of female misbehavior that can only be read as coherent if we see it as affirming freedom of personal choice by refusing to adhere to a single doctrine that defines what freedom properly means.

NOTES

1. Rosa Von Praunheim, interview by author, 1994.

2. Vincent Canby, Review of *It is Not the Homosexual Who is Perverse, But the Society in Which He Lives*, *The New York Times*, National Edition, v127, November 25, 1977: C-10.

3. Vindicating unusual characters is one of Von Praunheim's central concerns. In a recent interview, Von Praunheim noted:

> It's really gratifying when unusual people, types who are usually only laughed at, looked down on by the middle class, who are funny and unique, can be made accessible to large audiences through a careful mediation, like the one I try to provide through my films. It's important in our sterile society, which stresses only assimilation and adjustment, that as many people as possible witness just how intelligent, special and inspiring these outsiders are.

See Von Praunheim, quoted in Laurence A. Rickels, "It's a wound-erful life," *Artforum*, v32, December, 1993: 47.

4. According to film historian David Cook, Von Praunheim, born in 1942, changed his name from Holgar Mischwitzky to the name by which he is now known. See Cook, *A History of Narrative Film* (New York: W. W. Norton & Co., 1990), 870.

5. J. Hoberman, Review of *It is Not the Homosexual Who is Perverse, But the Situation in Which He Lives*, *Village Voice*, v22, Nov. 28, 1977: 51.

6. J. Hoberman, Review of *Army of Lovers*, *Village Voice*, v24, December 10, 1979: 61.

7. David Hansen, Review of *I Am My Own Woman*, *Variety*, v349, December 7, 1992: 72.

8. Stephen Holden, Review of *I Am My Own Woman*, *The New York Times*, National Edition, April 29, 1994, v143: C-15.

9. Julia Knight, "Off Our Backs," *Sight and Sound*, v2n2, June 1992: 30.

10. Manohla Dargis, Review. of *Female Misbehavior*, *Village Voice*, v38, April 27, 1993: 62.

11. Claire Monk, Review of *Verführung: Die Grausame Frau*, *Sight and Sound*, NS3, May, 1993: 59.

12. Sprinkle became the subject of considerable controversy when she applied to the NEA for funding as a performance artist. Under the troubled leadership of John Frohnmayer, the NEA came under attack when the Rev. John Wildmon and others publicly assailed the agency for funding what they considered the pornographic work of artists like Sprinkle and Karen Finley. For a detailed discussion of the controversy, see Steven C. Dubin, *Arresting Images: Impolitic Art and Uncivil Actions*, (London: Routledge, 1992), 125-58.

13. Manohla Dargis, in op. cit. 62, takes exactly this position on the character of Max, noting also of the portrayal of Paglia that it reveals a woman

who has negated femininity by making use of the strategies of patriarchy—
acting excessively aggressively—in the process of claiming political power.

14. Knight, 31.

CHAPTER 7

Conclusion

A recent episode of the television series *Friends* features a running joke in which one of the principal male characters, a twenty-something, regular guy, repeatedly happens upon two of his female friends while they are hugging. Mistaking the hugs for indications that the women are bisexual, the young man nods with approval as he watches, displaying on his face unqualified delight as he appears to fantasize his two lady friends having sex. The audience, having witnessed the events leading up to the hugs, knows that the women are, in fact, clearly heterosexual, that they are hugging each other in a gesture of purely platonic appreciation of one another. The whole matter is treated as a bit of harmless fun: the girls really are straight, and the young man is allowed to enjoy himself.

Perhaps without meaning to do so, the writers of this episode have performed a double erasure of homosexuality. Appropriated—for the umpteenth time—as an element of male pleasure, the idea of lesbian relationships is denied as being able (or being allowed) to exist for its own sake; appropriated as an element of ironic humor, the idea of lesbian sex is presented as being an error. The interesting thing to me about this presentation of homosexuality is that it is clearly meant to reflect an enlightened portrayal of a subject which, certainly in television, is still regarded as controversial. This case of mistaken identity is intended, we must guess, to make the notion of homosexuality more "user-friendly" to a contemporary audience, while the notion of female sexuality is safely framed within the context of male heterosexual pleasure.

Television has dealt with homosexuality at least as often as film in the last ten years, if not more so; it has also attempted more fully than film to present homosexuality fairly.[1] Television series such as *Melrose Place*, *The Nanny*, *Designing Women*, *L.A. Law*, *Roseanne*, *Ellen*, and *Frasier* are among only the most recent series on network television that have included significant, generally sympathetic lesbian and gay characters either as series regulars or as characters appearing for a single or a limited number of episodes. Even in the seventies television series such as *All in the Family*, *Maude*, and *Sanford and Son* showed the American viewing audience gay characters who were, by and large, just regular folks. I think it is significant here that most of what television has had to say about homosexual people has been framed within the context of situation comedies. While it may be good news that gay people have been presented more and more in mainstream media like television, it is nonetheless remarkable to note how much, over the last twenty-five years, the media have kept stories about gay people corralled within the relatively safe area of comedy. It certainly is a triumph for gay people to have gained more visibility in mainstream social life, and television comedy has been one of the most important agents making that visibility possible. The questions that arise for me here are these: Have gay people in contemporary comedies really come that far since being introduced as hapless sissies in thirties musical comedies, and can we expect to see more serious portrayals of gay people to complement the undeniable substance of what television shows like *Roseanne* have offered us?

It is encouraging to see that, in addition to regular series, television has presented special shows dealing in noncomedic narrative tropes with matters that concern lesbian and gay people. One such show is the special *Roommates* (1994), a story about a gay man with HIV, played by Eric Stoltz, who is obliged to become the roommate of a heterosexual man, portrayed by Randy Quaid, also stricken with the illness. Another special recently presented is *Serving in Silence: The Margarethe Cammermeyer Story* (1995), with actress Glenn Close playing the part of the prominent National Guard nurse who was forced to resign her commission after she told her superiors she was a lesbian. These special television films focus on portraying attempts by lesbian and gay people to bridge the gap of understanding with heterosexuals. Such shows tend to portray lesbians and gay men as being courageous, admirable, "everyday" people guided by principles with which most people would sympathize—principles of personal integrity and compassion. Certainly, these series and special shows aired recently on television mark enormous steps of progress towards creating and maintaining a dialogue regarding the many roles that gay people play in mainstream American life.

Presented on the Public Broadcasting System, other series and made-for-television films have dealt with adaptations of novels by gay authors that feature central lesbian and gay characters. One such film, *The Lost Language of Cranes* (released in 1993, adapted from David Leavitt's novel), follows a successful, young, happily gay man as he comes out to his family, who give him their support. The family falls into crisis, however, when it comes to light that the father, a closeted gay man, has been living a double life throughout his marriage. Leavitt's story is very well rendered in this film, most importantly in the way that the ethical benefits of living "out" in society are contrasted with the pain of living in the darkness—the young son who is openly gay is contrasted with the father whose life falls apart because he finds there isn't room enough even for him in the closet he has constructed. The film also does an excellent job of developing Leavitt's explication of the difficulty that gay people have of communicating a knowledge of their selves to the world around them. This explication takes the form of intercutting the stories of the father and son with a story of a young child who, as a result of having been locked away by cruel parents, has developed a complex language system. The child's story functions well as a comment most especially on the plight of the closeted gay man by indicating how deeply, even under the most adverse conditions, people seek to find a way of making contact with others using the tools that life gives them.

Tales of the City (adapted in 1994 as a four-part miniseries from the first of a group of novels by Armistead Maupin) chronicles the lives of a group of people—some of them gay, some of them bisexual and some of them straight— who converge and become friends and lovers in a seemingly enchanted boardinghouse (owned and operated by a woman who had been born a man) in San Francisco in the early 1970s. Striking a great balance between frankness and decorum, *Tales* is as appealing for the way it shows us in an honestly touching way the innocence of the best of the "me" generation was as it is for showing how startlingly different the sensibility of the seventies—the life and time of just one generation ago—is from that of the present.

These two films on PBS have offered viewers arguably the most extensively developed stories about homosexual people seen anywhere in the media of film or television, presenting gay characters as being, for the most part, healthy, more or less average people who go about building their lives in a loving, constructive way. It seems evident that such films, with their emphasis on showing gay people as ordinary people, are intended to further the notion that lesbians and gay men are already part of mainstream society.

As we can see that there has been a proliferation in the presentation of lesbian and gay characters on television and that the characters presented have generally been sympathetic, we must also note how problematic many of these presentations have been. When news spread in 1994 that we would see a lesbian kiss on *Roseanne* between Roseanne and Margaux Hemingway, series commercial sponsors threatened to withdraw their support unless the kissing scene was cut (this despite the fact that the series had already established two regular characters as homosexuals, portrayed by Sandra Bernhardt and Martin Mull). The series star and producer, Roseanne, refused to give in, the episode aired without censorship, and the firmament (as well as commercial sponsorship contracts) remained intact.

When PBS announced plans to air *Tales of the City*, a political war ensued, with powerful members of the political right excoriating the Corporation for Public Broadcasting for lending its support to a project which, in the view of the right, was inimical to American family values. Before the series aired (it should not be forgotten that the series was coproduced by a British film group,[2] as no domestic producer could be found to complete the project without assistance), church groups organized phone campaigns to flood local PBS affiliates with calls demanding that the series not be shown, and politicians, both local and national, threatened to cut further funding for PBS if the series was shown. When PBS aired the series in 1993, some local affiliate PBS stations did not pick it up. Other affiliated stations aired the series in a censored version (for content, since the series contained nude scenes—bare female breasts, bare male buttocks—and a kiss scene between two men; and for language, as the series dialogue employed most of the naughty old Anglo-Saxon body function monosyllables). The PBS affiliates that aired the unexpurgated version of the series included a disclaimer, displayed frequently throughout the series' four episodes, warning of the story's mature and possibly objectionable content.

After the series aired, public support and criticism poured into the offices of PBS and its affiliates, resulting in local government hearings, such as one held in Georgia, in which the directors of PBS were called on the carpet, scolded by lawmakers, and asked to defend the need for further government funding of public television. The director of the principal PBS affiliate in Georgia, Richard Ottinger of WGTV, was made the subject of a televised state congressional hearing in which he was soundly criticized for airing the series. Responding by defending the artistic and social merits of the series, Ottinger made no apologies for WGTV's choice in airing the series. Shortly after the furor subsided, however, Ottinger resigned his position, claiming that he did so without pressure from his superiors.

Clearly, the subject of homosexuality on television still makes a good number of powerful people uncomfortable. In the current political climate—the aftermath of the 1994 elections, in which roughly 36 percent of the American electorate delivered to the conservative political establishment a "mandate" to lead—the debate continues as to whether artistic projects that discuss homosexuality deserve public support. Indeed, the appearance of series such as *Tales* has fueled the political right's argument that public funding for PBS should be curtailed if not suspended altogether, and it is very doubtful that, in the United States at least, we will be seeing such stories in the near future. Ironically, former Secretary of Education William Bennett, an outspoken foe of public television, recently succeeded in getting PBS to broadcast an animated version of his book, *The Book of Virtues*. It appears very clear that, for the time being, PBS is going to have to toe the conservative, family-values line much more faithfully if it is going to keep its public funding.

Central to the furor over these series is the question, Should homosexuality as a way of living have a place in mainstream American values? As long as the question continues to be asked, lesbians and gay men must recognize that an answer is already being given: our position with respect to mainstream society is always contingently legitimate at best; we live, we must remember, at the margin of society.

The contingency of our position finds an analogue in a gay character regularly appearing on the *Melrose Place* television series. The character, Matt (portrayed by actor Doug Savant), is a nice guy: good-looking, likable, healthy, stable, and morally upright, he appears as a minor character who, unlike the rest of the series characters, never seems to get involved in shady business or romantic double dealings. While the series' other regular characters (principal among them the villainous minx portrayed by the actress Heather Locklear) hop from bed to bed in torrid love scenes, Matt has largely been left on the sidelines of the action, occasionally appearing in a parenthetical scene with a new boyfriend, seen hugging or kissing behind a curtain, or seen in full view as he shakes hands and says goodbye for the last time to his ex-boyfriend. Recently, after having appeared for several seasons on the show, Matt was finally allowed to have a boyfriend who didn't disappear after two episodes. While other characters in the series live trouble-filled (but fascinating) lives centered around long-running sexual misalliances, Matt remains a rather dull character by comparison to the other series regulars. The other regulars may be airheads, but at least they're interesting. On the one hand, the series depicts heterosexuals as madly bed-hopping partygoers chronically infected, perhaps anachronistically, with a syndrome reflecting 1970s values: Saturday Night Fever. On the other hand, the series depicts homosexuals (more accurately, *the* homosexual) even more anachronistically as admirable, if irrelevant, nonentities leading a largely safe, contemplative life. Ineluctably, the message implicit in this arrangement is that as long as he remains on the edge of things, making no false moves and staying fully clothed, the homosexual may retain his place at the table.

All that we have noted about the appearance of homosexual characters in television reveals how upsetting the image of the homosexual is to mainstream society. When in the mid-nineties an artist presents images of lesbians or gay men before the public, she runs the risk of angering or disaffecting someone with the power to cause trouble. In the late nineties, a quarter century after Stonewall, publicly distributed images of homosexuals are still dangerous. Under the best of circumstances, the image of the homosexual in television is accepted by the public without much difficulty, as long as that image is partially erased by representing the homosexual as being divested of his or her sexual character. Depicting lesbians and gay men as sexual people is still, it seems, exposing a dirty secret, like the bed sheets displayed at Oscar Wilde's trial. It is, however, important for us to make note of the "baseline" values of acceptability that images of homosexuality in television represent. Having defined the rules of acceptability as it has, perhaps television gives us the most comprehensive sense of what images of homosexual people mean today in mainstream society.

Perhaps, one might respond, matters are not so bleak as I have indicated. After all, *Tales of the City* aired in many parts of the country in its entirety, and it received a great deal of public and critical support, including an Emmy nomination. The series has been released as a video set, and you can find it at Blockbuster if you're interested. While these things are true, it is also true that plans to produce a sequel have been, as of the present date, abandoned, owing to the controversy arising from the original project's airing.[3] *Serving in Silence: The Margarethe Cammermeyer Story*, one might add, aired over commercial television to wide acclaim. This also is true, but it must be noted that the series aired despite the efforts of the United States Army to have the series shelved. It should also be noted that the series was produced by Barbra Streisand and a partnership of independent gay television producers[4]: What does it suggest about the affections of mainstream television producers that the Cammermeyer project was funded by a partnership assembled largely by a wealthy artist long noted for her willingness to tell the rest of Hollywood to go to hell? The television projects discussed here focus, we must remember, on very mild portrayals of homosexuals as sexual people: they have no explicit sex scenes between same-sex couples, and they portray characters who are generally white, middle-class people. The simple fact remains that even such "benign" images of homosexuals must run a very difficult gauntlet of political scrutiny before they are allowed to come before the public. It the best of cases, in the mildest of forms, in the tamest of media, it is still, in the mid-nineties, difficult to get to see images of lesbians and gay men.

Meanwhile, the media of fictional film and television continue to present seriously troublesome images relating to homosexuals. In a *Saturday Night Live* television sketch that aired not all that long ago, for instance, a running joke involves homosexuality and vampirism. In the sketch John Travolta, playing the part of Dracula, tries to scare a couple—a young man and woman—who stray into his castle. Dracula/Travolta attempts to scare the couple by displaying his powers as a vampire. The couple, in turn, attribute his eeriness to being gay, not to being a vampire. Discerning this misunderstanding, Dracula is horrified; he tries to reassure the couple that he is a "normal" vampire, not a queer one. His efforts collapse, however, when his associate Renfield and his neighbor the Wolf Man enter the scene. Portrayed as stereotypically effeminate queens, Renfield and the Wolf Man create the impression that Dracula is also gay (a good, old-fashioned case of guilt by association). Suspecting this relationship, the couple refuses to be convinced that Dracula is straight, and the sketch ends with Dracula dithering in frustration. The sketch appears to drive home the point that, at the very least, being thought of as a vampire is not a problem, while being thought of as a homosexual is intolerable. The tenor of the sketch is such that we cannot say with certainty whether the writers intended for us to sympathize with Renfield and the Wolf Man, two happily queer monsters, or with Dracula, the monster angry at the slanderous attack on his dignity.

Another troubling episode relating to gays and image production is the unfolding story of the planned project for a film about Harvey Milk, the gay San Francisco supervisor who, together with San Francisco Mayor John Moscone, was murdered by ousted city supervisor Dan White. The film was to be made from the late Randy Shilts's book on Harvey Milk, *The Mayor of Castro Street*. When it was announced that the film would be directed by Oliver Stone, the gay press virtually exploded in protest. How, it was asked, could the man who directed JFK—with its gaggle of vicious, seditious, terrorist drag queens and hustlers, all of them portrayed by big-time Hollywood tough guys—direct a film about one of gay liberation's unqualified heroes? After Stone parried for a few months with the press, the project, which has major studio backing, was turned over to openly gay director Gus Van Sant. The project, however, has been languishing as a work-in-progress for well over a year now without a complete cast.[5] Luckily, audiences already have a document of Milk's remarkable life in *The Times of Harvey Milk*, an excellent documentary released in 1984 by independent gay director Robert Epstein. Though the planned studio film about Milk may ultimately prove to be irrelevant, the fact that it has had so much difficulty being completed is not. In the best of circumstances, with the most mainstream funding source, with the best of stories, homosexual characters are still in danger of being erased in the media.

Even if we look at recent films that do cater to a gay audience, we find some puzzling if not disturbing facts relating to how gay people show up in film. For instance, two of the biggest box-office draws of 1995 and 1996 were films that dealt with gay characters, *The Bird Cage* and *To Wong Foo, Thanks for Everything, Julie Newmar*. Both films were big-budget Hollywood productions featuring major directors (Mike Nichols) and major stars (Patrick Swayze). What I find so disturbing about these two films is that the whole idea of their success is based on the safety of the material they employ. *Bird Cage* is a virtual word-by-word rewrite of the cult classic *La Cage aux Folles*, a film that has been around for twenty years, has had two bad sequels, and has been recycled as a Broadway musical. *To Wong Foo* is another recycling effort, based on the highly successful Australian film *Priscilla, Queen of the Desert*. In the case of both films, it seems clear that the post-*Waterworld* film industry saw itself as cashing in on the "gay market" by pouring bundles of money into can't-miss projects. The message Hollywood seems to sending here is that we're willing to risk money on a gay-themed project as long as it doesn't do anything new. Where does that leave the public, and where does it leave gay people? In the past, driven up a Forrest Gumpstunk.

Elsewhere among the big-budget movies, there are a few—very few—compelling images of gay people that partake of the darker qualities of real human power. David Cronenberg's admittedly homo-ambivalent *Naked Lunch* presents the peripheral characters of William Burroughs's dark satire as being compellingly dark, powerfully monstrous (or monstrously powerful) creatures, while rendering the central character, Burroughs himself, as a somewhat disappointingly whitewashed, more or less regular guy (as far as junkie writers go). More interesting and far more successful is Neil Jordan's much criticized version of Anne Rice's novel, *Interview With the Vampire*. Jordan's film suffered—or should I say profited?—from a good deal of gay-media-activist criticism (as well as initial criticism from author Rice) because the director chose Tom Cruise—long accused by various gay media mavens of being a closet queen—to play the part of the Vampire Lestat. Because Lestat the literary character had become a cult figure among gay and straight readers alike, and because he was one of the most intensely homoerotic figures to have appeared in popular culture, a sizable portion of the public essentially fed interest in the film before it ever opened by predicting that Cruise, viewed as too lightweight an actor for the part and as a traitor to the gay community, would turn the movie into a flop. In fact, Jordan and Cruise succeeded in bringing Lestat into view with all of the menace and charisma one hopes for in a good monster. Fully possessing the complexity of a character invested with a monumental reservoir of passion, Cruise's Lestat plays compellingly opposite Brad Pitt's (chronically kvetching) Louis in an expression of homoerotic desire as a romance between consciousness and darkness. In accomplishing this, Jordan's film and Cruise's portrayal succeed at creating a universal myth for romance—isn't romance always a journey through some sort of madness?—that focuses strongly and creatively on homosexual identity. Perhaps *Interview With the Vampire* illustrates as no other recent film has how rich are the possibilities of creating cinematic narratives that explore the power of darkness inherent to homosexuality.

All of the foregoing discussion will serve, I hope, to underscore something about the films the present study has discussed in detail. Perhaps only by looking at what, as of the present writing, the rest of the media do to and with homosexuals can one begin to understand why certain adventuresome filmmakers would choose to make such dark, eccentric films about homosexuals as have Van Sant, araki, Genet, Fassbinder, Von Praunheim, and Treut. What these films do is to perform a violently corrective reinscription of the image of the homosexual into a media environment that all too often, either casually or with malice, erases those images.

As I see it, the films presented in the body of the present study reinscribe the image of the homosexual in either one of two ways: by presenting the homosexual as being already part of the dominant heterosexual social order; or by violently asserting the alterity of homosexuals with respect to the dominant order, conceiving that alterity as a desirable state of being. Neither species of film, I would maintain, seeks to reclaim or assimilate homosexuality as a value contributing to the dominant social order's legitimacy. On the contrary, both species comment on dominant order's fundamental perversity.

Consider, for example, how homosexual desire is presented in *A Song of Love*, *Querelle*, and *My Own Private Idaho*. In these films homosexuality is presented as a form of lawlessness, but that form always works by support of or in collusion with the dominant order. This order is conceived either as the order of social law (the prison and the warder in *A Song of Love* or the police in *Querelle*) or as the order of the father (Scott's father and Mike's search for a father *in My Own Private Idaho*). In these films, the homosexual appears on the surface to be an "outcast," a social monster who appears to affront or endanger the values of the dominant order. Closer inspection reveals, however, that the outcast's perverse behavior is bound up with his use of the dominant order to claim a position of social power. For example, in *A Song of Love* the prisoner known as the murderer derives power from using his condition of confinement to maintain and intensify his own transgressive pleasure. The prison walls between his cellmate and himself, and between the sexually aroused warder and himself, allow his pleasure to remain intact. Thus the law itself contributes to the conditions that allow the prisoner's transgressive pleasure to exist, and the prisoner gains a certain freedom within the prison by revealing how the law colludes with his transgressive desire.

Similarly, in *Querelle* we see significant signs that the dominant, ostensibly heterosexual male order is always implicated in the perversity of homosexual transgression. Mario the policeman, for instance, works in collusion with Nono the homosexual whoremonger: the law works with, not in spite of, the criminal sexual underground. The character Querelle, the central figure in which archetypal masculinity is conjoined with homosexual passivity and monstrous criminality, ends up "married," at the conclusion of the film, to an unassailably stable figure of the dominant male order, Lt. Seblon. In Fassbinder's formulation of values, the monstrous homosexual is, from beginning to end, inscribed in the dominant male order.

And finally, *My Own Private Idaho* presents the gay man as a social monster inevitably connected with the order of the father. The character Scott conducts his journey through perversity so as to solidify his position with respect to his biological father: by erring, he makes his redemption possible. By denying his perverse father, Bob, the character Scott affirms both his own perverse nature (by denying his authentic life as a hustler) and his position in the traditional male hierarchy—a hierarchy presented in the film as being part of his legal inheritance.

In all three of these films, the dominant male order is exposed rather than questioned. These films do not appear to provide room for us to ask polemical questions about whether the order of things should be changed; rather, they seem to focus on making ontological observations about the nature of the order of male values. In all three films, what is being said most centrally is that the dominant structure of heterosexual male identification creates the conditions in which homosexual desire is possible. What is exposed here is the secret that the law, by creating the pervert, creates not a helpless outsider, but rather a certain type of actually rather powerful player who, by virtue of his status as a pervert, enjoys a position of privilege within the dominant male hierarchy. The power that the pervert enjoys lies in the fact that he serves as a sign, a monstrum, that there is no difference between one side of the law and the other, no difference between the fairy and the regular guy.

Read in perhaps the most radical way, the arguments of the three films mentioned above use the figure of the socially monstrous homosexual to erase the opposition between normalcy and deviance in the dominant social order. If, by doing so, they manage to deconstruct the system of values in that order, they do not seem to point clearly to the idea that another social order, another way of defining maleness, is either possible or desirable. The more recent films discussed here, however—*The Living End, Poison, I Am My Own Woman*, and *Female Misbehavior*—attempt to employ the figure of the monstrous homosexual as a sign pointing the way out of the dominant male order of values. By pointing out an exit route, these films appear to invite the audience to imagine queer values of identity, values of identity not taken from or working with the status quo.

Of the four films listed in this last group, three of them present the trope of killing or escaping from the mainstream world, a world envisaged as the order of the father. In *The Living End*, Luke commits several murders and enlists Jon as his accomplice, thus making it impossible for either man to return to a normal life. A metaphor for the irrevocability of HIV infection, these murders are also metaphors for the indefensibility of homophobia. In *Poison*, Richie Beacon's murdering his father plays as a counterpoint to Broom and Bolton's status as condemned men. Richie himself, invested in the film with homoerotic character, murders his father and miraculously flies away. Unable to fit into the world around him, Richie escapes. Jack, the condemned criminal and the victim of homophobia, dies as he tries to escape. *I Am My Own Woman* gives us a document of an actual parricide: the account of the murder of Lottchen's father inclines us to sympathize with the murderer, who killed his abusive father to prevent the latter from killing the family. In these films, escaping the order of the law, the order of the father, is desirable; succeeding at doing so is a triumph.

If, taken as a group, this last set of films points the way to a type of sexual identification outside the order of the father, it appears clear that the films in this group subdivide into two smaller groups: films that point the way out and films that give us a view of life on the outside. Where *Poison* or *The Living End* tracks queer identity on its way out of mainstream society, *I Am My Own Woman* and *Female Misbehavior* show us contented life on the outside. Von Praunheim's Lottchen is a squatter: she takes up residence in ruins and creates her own world there. Contentedly perverse, Lottchen has created a world of balance from a heap of trash. In a very different way, the women of *Female Misbehavior* have abandoned the world of the father by constructing their identities resolutely in terms of their own pleasure. Treut's Dr. Paglia is a monument unto herself, a monument through which silliness and certainty proclaim themselves as partners in Paglia's use of the world as her playground. Annie Sprinkle emerges in the film as a sort of living temple, a female sexual being in rapt contemplation of itself, indifferent to the male gaze. In Sprinkle's one-woman cult, perverse playfulness is an act of adoration performed between the female body as celebrant, as temple and as liturgical text. The woman presented in *Bondage*, like Sprinkle, has focused her life around a true lesbian separatist's view that women find growth and fulfillment through other women; maleness, in this woman's world, is simply irrelevant. Even Treut's character Max, I would argue, shows us a person contentedly living in the world outside, the queer world. Clearly, in Treut's film Max's contentment with his physical reconstruction as a man is valorized as being an indication of health, of constructive personal awareness. If we can take Max at his word, his construction of himself as a man is not so much a repudiation of femininity as it is a realization that his identity is centered in his own individual consciousness, not in the absolute truths of external natural law.

In concluding, I would say that all the films we have examined in detail here comment radically on the idea of the assimilation of gays and lesbians into mainstream society. *A Song of Love*, *Querelle*, and *Idaho* speak to gay assimilationists and straight people alike by saying: The person you have imagined as a monster, an outsider, is an integral part of the system of values you use to define normalcy. Homosexual men, these films indicate, are not outsiders at all; they are, rather, the individuals who express most archetypically the received notion of what a real man is. Thus, for gays to speak of the need for us to assimilate into mainstream society is to speak nonsense: we are already there, holy icons at the center of patriarchy. The more recent films—by araki, Haynes, Von Praunheim and Treut— point in a very different direction. Where a film like *Querelle* finally exhibits a deep political pessimism, revealing the lie embedded within the dominant order, a film like *I Am My Own Woman* finally posits a sense of idealistic optimism by inviting gay people to see that it is possible to live happily, like Charlotte Von Mahlsdorf, among the ruins. Idealism is also implied in the miraculous nature of Richie Beacon's flight in *Poison*. This sense of idealism, however troubled (as in *The Living End*) by homophobia and AIDS, challenges gay people to imagine a way to build their lives without seeking validation from the dominant social order, or as arch-queen Quentin Crisp said somewhere, "Never mind keeping up with the Joneses; drag them down to your level—it's cheaper."

Anyone who has kept up long enough to be reading the present sentence has a perfectly good right to ask, Just what is it you want? I have inveighed against Hollywood's mass production of sissies, its refusal to give us queers much air time, and I've come to the defense of characters whom I myself quite possibly would be nervous to have as neighbors. Of course, my point here has been not at all to provide anyone with something like a precise recipe for living—I don't propose that anyone who might have read these pages go out and sell his or her body or that the queers of any country rise up and take arms (at least, perhaps, not just yet). What I have been suggesting here has everything to do with real life, but only insofar as real life is directed by the imagination. It occurs to me that, particularly in a time that has become so fully governed by an idea as odious as political correctness, it is important for us—at the very least—to examine both how much of our interior lives we leave unlived and how much that lack costs us. I believe, very much as a result of my own personal experience but also on the basis of what I have seen and heard from those close to me—both gay and straight—that we are at a time of crisis in which we have come to surrender part of our individual power in an effort to pay what must certainly only be lip service to a spirit of the times that tells us we must all be normal, whatever that is. The monsters of our imagination, I think, point towards a corrective device that we can use to live.

The search for normalcy—I should say the highly puritanical insistence upon it—has seeped into virtually every arena of public and private life to such a degree that I wonder if there is any hope left for us. The idea of inclusiveness, I'm afraid, is really all too often a rather mean-spirited attempt at teaching people how to ignore what they really find offensive. Indeed, that may be all that can be expected of the greater number of people, but I would like to raise a voice in exception to what I myself find, finally, to be an intolerably pessimistic assumption about the potential of human consciousness. What I would rather see than a complex of manners rising up around the mantra "never mind" is an admission that it does matter very much that we keep reminding ourselves to see all that is dark and objectionable in ourselves, most importantly, and in others, secondly, without taking up arms precipitously and without legislating brutally against all that we find to be dark.

I would regard it as a signal indication of health in our culture, especially the culture of queer people, if we could tolerate more images like the ones I have labored over here. It would give me great hope to see a gay version of *Dracula* that isn't simply porn, or a gay Frankenstein version that isn't a camp musical. I would like to see more Lestats, more Lottchens, more Nadjas. The greatest opposition to the creation of such apparitions could be, I think, gay people themselves, so caught up in the ample gains they've made socially over the past quarter century: Just shut up and drive! On the backs of the bull daggers, drag queens, and leather freaks who got their heads knocked in at Stonewall, gay and lesbian suburbanites ride home from work every day, not noticing much, not caring, perhaps giving up more of themselves than they need to. As we assimilate into everyday life, we forget the power we have to disturb others—and ourselves—by claiming our birthright, which is our proximity to the edge of things. If we can maintain at least some of our irritating edginess, we reflect back on the center of things and make it look out towards us. If the center turns ever inward, it sees nothing, not even itself. The one thing our monsters tell us is that we must continue to look at our darkness and learn how to use it. The monsters we have been accused of being, and the monsters we really are, hidden in our tract houses, our seamless lives, challenge us to remember the things we are inclined too easily to surrender.

NOTES

1. See in particular Vito Russo's assessment of homosexuality in television in *op. cit.*, 221. Although Russo died in September 1990, his last public appraisal of the depiction of gay people in the movies and on television describes the present situation fairly accurately.

2. This was the British production group *Propaganda/Working Title*, which produced the series in conjunction with another British group, *Channel Four*; together the two British sources worked to produce the series in conjunction with funding from the National Endowment for the Arts, the Corporation for Public Broadcasting, and author Armistead Maupin. The series aired under the sponsorship of PBS affiliate KQED of San Francisco and of PBS's *American Playhouse* series, a series designed to showcase works of dramatic art by major contemporary artists. It should be noted, furthermore, that the series featured a British director, Alistair Reid, and a number of British actors in the principal roles, one of which was that of a young gay man from Florida who spoke with a Southern drawl. All in all, the series would not have been completed without the substantial support of creative and financial sources from outside the United States. We should also note that *The Lost Language of Cranes* was produced in part and directed by sources foreign to the United States: coproduced by BBC-TV and New York City's Thirteen-WNET, it was directed by British director Nigel Finch and was shot largely in Great Britain with a mostly British cast.

3. Greenberg, "No More Tales," 59.

4. Charles Isherwood, "The Men Behind Glenn," *The Advocate*, Issue 672/673, January 24, 1995: 71.

5. For a detailed discussion of the chaos surrounding the filming of *The Mayor of Castro Street*, see Isherwood, 71.

Appendix: An Interview With Todd Haynes

Following is a transcript of a phone interview I conducted with Todd Haynes on 16 January, 1995. In the text, "*T*" refers to Mr. Haynes, and "*M*" refers to Michael Saunders. In redacting this interview, I have attempted to keep the transcript as close to being a word-for-word account as my typing abilities will allow. Inevitably, this attempt will convey to the reader both my own verbal sloppiness and the extraordinary elegance and acute focus of Mr. Haynes's conversation. I apologize to the readers for asking them to endure the former, and I am pleased to be able to present evidence of the latter.

M. To begin with, what I'm doing with this work is I'm looking at images of homosexual characters as monsters in film. So my departure point is first backing up and asking some questions and getting some things in the foreground of my awareness as I think about all this and trying to see how I want to define homosexuality in terms of monstrosity from the beginning and play with that idea. And it seems that, when I try to put all of what I know about homosexuality and monstrosity and images together, my departure point is this: namely, that traditional culture tends to view homosexuality as monstrous in two senses: first as a deformation of the natural order as defined by sexuality, as defined by expressions of relationships—human relationships—in the first sense, as a kind of deformation; and in the second sense, as a kind of omen: homosexuality tends to be viewed in conservative culture which, now frighteningly seems to be reasserting itself, but it tends to get viewed as a form of expression or living that is doomed. The homosexual gets viewed very often as being a person who is doomed to undo himself, and as such serves as an omen: look what will happen to you if you deviate from the natural order. So those are the two basic senses in which I'm beginning to try to play with the whole idea of how I think homosexuality works in terms of talking about monstrosity. What I get to after that is, given the strength with which this sense of the homosexual as monster and the variety of senses with which that sense expresses itself in the culture, it seems interesting to look at images, particularly images—not just defined as visual images but images in any sense, images in writing, for instance— but where images of the homosexual as monster tend to come up. So here I'm crash landing into my first question for you: How do you see those images coming up in film? Does it seem to you that such images are a significant part of film imagery?

T. Yes, definitely, especially in the way that you just defined monstrousness. Do you want to name a couple of films or a range of films that you might be talking about or have already talked about in your dissertation?

M. Basically I'm dividing film into—I'm trying to gather a cluster of what probably most people talking now would consider new queer cinema on the one hand, and setting that as the focal point of my analyses—what I'm actually doing readings of in the dissertation—setting that on one side and looking at what I'm vaguely and probably sloppily calling traditional cinema on the other hand.

T. I'm just thinking really off the top of my head of films like—and you should tell me if these are films you've thought about or not—*The Living End* or *Swoon*, even *My Own Private Idaho*, which still had one step in mainstream production probably more than the others.

M. *Querelle*?

T. Fassbinder's *Querelle* and what else?

M. The granddaddy for me is Genet's *A Song of Love*, and Kenneth Anger—*Fireworks* and *Scorpio Rising* and all those other things. So Genet is the granddaddy and then you—with a quiet underground in the form of people like Kenneth Anger, you move forward into the sixties and seventies, then comes Fassbinder with a bang in movies like *Fox and His Friends* and *The Bitter Tears of Petra Von Kant*, and finally *Querelle* and all the other films of his that deal with homosexuality or that feature homosexual characters. I'm also including films like Jarman's *Edward the Second*, Almodovar's *The Law of Desire*, a film by Agustin Villaronga called *In a Glass Cage*; Rosa Von Praunheim, his films, Jennie Livingston's film *Paris Is Burning*, Monika Treut's film *Female Misbehavior*, some of her other documentaries. So there's the pack that I want to look at, with you in that pack, on the one hand.

T. Yeah. I would definitely see elements of—when you first described those two aspects of monstrousness and applied them to the way gay characters are portrayed, I thought of how that certainly is true of more mainstream depictions of homosexuals in film, where they are often not the agents of the narrative in the way that they might be in some of the queer productions—films by gay filmmakers that come from the margins more than from the mainstream. And yet I think that you could probably find that both of the two aspects that you brought up—the sort of deformation or redrawing of traditional relationships, and then the kind of doomed element—would probably come up in various ways in both categories. I just think that there is a level at which the gay film-maker is purposely manipulating tropes that are both already constructed by the culture and circulating within the culture and activating them in various ways, but maybe without some of the corrective or cautionary elements that you will usually find in more mainstream productions, where it's necessary that the gay character dies or it's necessary that they're drawn as somewhat—that whatever those images are contrasted to within those films, that they're slotted in a more derogatory or more threatening category. But all the films that you're talking about from queer cinema seem to me to be ones which, under the banner of Genet himself, are films that aren't striving to, quote unquote, "reform" and create positive images of homosexuals and happy narratives in which everyone walks off in the sunset at the end, but instead where these tensions and these threats—the monstrousness of homosexuality per se is maintained and utilized. And that's certainly a tradition that I've come from or studied or find myself associated with.

M. And in so many ways that's a very dangerous thing for a filmmaker like you to be doing. I mean, you get things like the flak that you caught over *Poison*, the response to the "gobbing" scene at Sundance that's sort of become part of the myth of the film. Working with that kind of image puts you in a very dangerous position, it seems to me, from all sides.

T. Yeah. I agree, and yet what's funny when I think back to that whole pe-riod—it was strange that very few people from the right, or places where the film was getting its strongest criticism, said, See, the film simply proves that homosexuals are monsters and that there is this self-hatred of homosexuals—it's all there, this is a total indictment of the homosexual life from a homosexual case in point. Instead, the film seemed to generate the same anxieties about ho-mosexuality itself that the film was absolutely trying to talk about and in fact preserve. In other words, whatever anxieties homosexuality continues to unleash to mainstream society, I felt like my film was absolutely serving to do that for these people, and so you watched it being played out in their own range of anxieties, fears, denials and obsessions and all of that more than you saw it be-ing taken out on me, the homosexual. And in some weird way—I don't quite know why that happened—it happened exactly as I would have hoped.

M. From the other side of that, then, though, do you feel in your experience of the film after the fact, you may have gotten into a tight spot with gay people who said, Now wait a minute, what are you doing here, Mr. Haynes, do we need this?

T. Yeah, that did happen, it did come up, and I imagine that those feelings and mistrust of my film were felt even more strongly than was communicated to me directly. It did come up now and then, and I guess I was supported by a critical rethinking of the questions about positive imagery and identity politics that were circulating then and now, and in many ways there was always full critical support of the kinds of issues I was raising in the film. I think people often shouted down the poor questioners in an audience who would say, Why is it so negative? There were certainly screenings that I attended where that came up.

M. In choosing to go back to Genet, in choosing to mine him for things to do, for things to say about all these issues...Genet seems to focus so intensely on the notion of abjection, this extremely spiritual sense of the meaning of abjection, and of course that does show up in *Poison*, the process and the whole experience of abjection, in a number of really different ways. Do you see yourself, among other things, as reading Genet's four-novel discussion of abjection; do you see yourself as reading that or responding to it? Are you recreating your sense of what Genet does with the idea of abjection in the film, either with respect to gay people or with respect to people in general?

T. I'm not sure if this exactly answers your question, but I definitely feel a dual reaction to those issues in Genet's work and in his general philosophies and that is, on the one hand, feeling this innate understanding of what he's talking about and identification with it and maybe even more a sense that it's describing a kind of isolation or antisocialism that I've always felt at some basic level. But, at the same time, it completely challenges me in what then feels like my complete assimilation in the world and in the evil society that he so much more fully distanced himself from than I do mine. And so I am both encouraged and completely fascinated by it, but at the same time I feel chastised by it as well, and almost, what he once said about André Gide's work and life, that he was of questionable immorality. I feel the same question placed on myself. And it challenges me, but I don't feel that I've failed and that I'm wrong, but that I'm encouraged to look at our culture with the same kinds of absolute suspicions that he did his; that it's a source of strength to turn to and that *Poison* has a strange kind of fixation on abjection, almost from the scatological—it's almost a science experiment of various body fluids. I mean, I've looked at the film and it's almost obsessed in a juvenile way with blood and guts and spit and shit, all of these literal versions of abjection. But those are the markers that differentiate the characters from the world in which they live, so naturally the film would focus on those pieces of evidence.

M. Then I'm led to another question, and it's this: does that abjection into which these characters are thrown or into which they're born or whatever, does that describe a position of power or does it describe a condition of being defeated from the very beginning?

T. No, I don't think it describes a position of being defeated from the very beginning in the slightest, in fact. But it's not solely a position of power. It's certainly not just a position of power that they discover in this acknowledgment or even in this celebration of that abjection. I think it's much more a position of—it's a dual position of masochistic power. Because abjection is part of every body—every internal body is full of the same fluids and juices and excrements that the characters in *Poison* either emit onto one another or are the subject of the abuse of language and fluids and abjection from other characters or from the society around them. But I guess to me it's something that singles them out as these marked bodies [who] are different from the world in which they live, but who are in the process of articulating that relationship to their respective societies and, in the act of that articulation, do become powerful and threatening to the society, but without that articulation are mere victims of the society. And so I think it's in the process of the realization and the understanding and the acknowledgment of those differences and the ways in which they're played out or literalized in these acts of horror—bodily instances of horror—that we all share, but that have a particular importance and meaning to these people and their lives that makes them into something more, and that is probably more on the line of powerful than not by the end. Or at least you see it being enacted differently—the distinction between the character Broom and the character Bolton: Bolton, who is ultimately acted upon by the people around him, is in a different relationship with respect to his society than Broom, in that he can't speak about his homosexuality, he can't articulate this desire. It's in him but he's not able to express it, and so he becomes this symbolic subject of masochistic pleasure, basically, that doesn't, maybe, transcend the world. Broom watching Bolton being spat upon is the way in which that image becomes something more than it is, through his watching of it; it's not simply the act itself, it's somebody transcribing it in their minds and transforming it as Genet did in *Miracle of the Rose* into something of an ecstatic nature. Without that, it would just be an act of abuse.

M. Just to be sure I haven't overread—are you comfortable with my talking about the characters in *Poison* as monsters? I tend to look at Richie as being a kind of monster in that he's a prodigy—he's referred to as a gift from God. Of course, Dr. Graves, I suppose there's not too much of a problem with seeing him as a monster. When you get to Jack and John, essentially you're talking about monstrosity as sociopathy, monstrosity as gay men, and linking up with sociopathy and all that.

T. I guess one thought is ... initially that there's a tradition in which monsters have been depicted in film and sometimes that tradition links up with the way traditional film deals with homosexuality. I think you're bringing up all these different uses of the monster, not necessarily derogatory or negative ways of discussing monstrousness or abjection. And *Poison* has all of it, almost every variant, every application is found within the various stories. I intended the "Horror" story to be more about the way traditional film—[presents] morality in traditional depictions of the monster—and applying that to depictions of people with AIDS or people with disease that I became very sensitive to around the time I was writing the film, where I saw the same kinds of moral divisions between the monstrous AIDS patient and the safe subjects watching these stories as I saw in traditional horror films. It's just that we have this great historical distance from the moral positions of the classic horror films, and so we can laugh about it, we can see the distinctions between the monster and the safe public as more absurd or ironic or funny or over the top or whatever. But, in the midst of your own history, you often don't see that. So I was trying to apply that to a more contemporary situation. So it's not about the Genet appropriation of monstrous terminology and his attempts to turn it around against the society and not having the society have the final word in those representations—which was, I think, more in the "Homo" section.

M. As I think about and look at all this, one of the things that finally seems to come out about monsters is how completely ambivalent our reaction to them tends to be. On the surface, they're disgusting things, but, of course, there's obviously something wonderfully exciting and fascinating about them. We keep bringing them back to life after we kill them, you know? The sequel business will never end.

T. That's so true. I think what's fascinating is the pleasure of being scared that's so evident in our history, in our culture. Mainstream film and mainstream novels are so fully aware of that market, that desire, the pleasure we feel in being terrified. I think it's a great analogy for homophobia. At times you are just shocked at how obsessive heterosexual society is about homosexuality, how incredibly sidetracked it can become with something that [it] shouldn't ultimately. If it's really so marginal, if it's really such a small percentage of the mainstream and so negligible, then why would they care? But there's this deep fascination with it that, obviously, has to do with what's inside every person, that is a great analogy for the intense fascination and pleasure that we feel being scared or being upset.

M. It's exciting. Someone quoted recently to me, and I don't know if I'm mangling the quote, but: People have imagined all kinds of really interesting hells, but no one has yet to come up with a heaven that anyone with any great sensibilities would want to live in. Horrific images have a great deal of charm. Finally, not to take too terribly much more of your time, I have a few questions about how you assembled *Poison*. Were you very much aware of *A Song of Love* when you were thinking about the film, or did it provide you with any kind of model for the film?

T. Actually not. I had seen it before making *Poison*, but it had been several years before, and there was a point where I wanted the director of photography, Maryse Alberti, to see it—she hadn't seen it before. We couldn't get a print, no one had a tape, and I thought well, maybe it's just as well that we embark on it without too much attention to its detail. It would invariably have a huge effect on me and would probably make me feel awful about anything that I would come up with. So, let it go, you know? Let it be the vague memory. But, in terms of its structure, it didn't have any direct effect on *Poison*. There are just scenes in it that you'll never get out of your head, and I remembered them when writing the film—the scene where Broom is kissing his hand in prison reminds me of some of those images of the wall and the smoke and stuff like that, but beyond that there isn't a real close analogy that I'm aware of.

M. How did the whole strategy of the intercutting stories evolve, or can you say how it evolved? Was it sort of an organic decision?

T. I knew that it was something I wanted to expand upon from previous films I've made and from the structure in Genet, the structure of *Our Lady of the Flowers* or *Funeral Rites* that, *Funeral Rites* particularly, have these very distinctive stories that are linked. *Our Lady of the Flowers* is more fluid, but still, the way he's constantly paralleling different stories, I wanted to incorporate that in the film. But it was also something I had done a little bit in *Superstar*, the film I made about Karen Carpenter that at least used different stylistic narrative forms, although also in the same story: they would go into this constructed documentary section or this more subjective montage style, and then it would be the doll, the fictional-star story-doll parts. But I was pleased to see how audiences could easily jump from one narrative trope to another, and I wanted to see what would happen if that was taken even further. And, if the different styles told different stories as well, sort of force the viewer to interpret the film as it went along. I always like to try to force them to do something while they're sitting there in the theater. The original script was intercut, because I wanted people who read the finished script to get a sense of what it would be like, the finished film; but I knew that it would change, it would have to change, the suggested points of intersection that the script reflected. Although a couple remained or they were embedded in the way we actually shot the scenes, and they made a narrative sense that persisted throughout the editing of the film. But really the film, which is so much about editing itself, needed to be open to that process to the greatest extent that it could be and so, when I cut the film with Jim Lyons, we really rewrote it and reconceived it in the process in many ways. So I think it really happened in the editing room. And it was a long editing process, which it needed to be, and I don't regret a day of it; it was really necessary to continually rethink it and reshape it and make it streamlined in the process of intercutting. It took a while to keep simply the dramatic tensions from one story alive while cutting into the next; at certain points you want to cut them off, but more often than not, I wanted to think of ways that that energy would just continue into the next story and inform what was happening to that story or add to the tensions that we left with the next story when we last saw it. So, it was hard, but it was certainly worth it.

M. My last question: Do you see yourself as either being shaped by or somehow in line with or proximate to other people that are identified now with new queer cinema, both in terms of the appropriation of the notion of queerness and all that that implies? Is that very much a part of what you're doing in your work or did you park it once you got finished with *Poison* or was it never any part of your work, really?

T. Well, as opposed to feeling part of a current cinematic movement among gay filmmakers, I would think that my films are more uniformly affected right now by AIDS than they are by what's happening among other gay filmmakers at this moment, and it's arguable that their films and perhaps even mainstream Hollywood films are equally affected by AIDS; maybe that's actually the thing that we are all, in various ways, working out. The film I've just completed, called *Safe*, which is my second feature after *Poison*—it took quite a while to get it made— doesn't have gay themes in it at all. The film is completely about illness and immunity, basically. And so, if there's any universal theme in all my films, it seems to be disease, so far. And, I hope that changes, but I have a feeling it may not until things change in the world; but I am really happy to see, almost without it being a conscious construction—I don't think it is that much more so, by other gay filmmakers—that the work that is coming out shares a criticism of mainstream culture that goes beyond content and that does affect forms and the ways in which characters are constructed and the ways in which our sympathies and our identification are complicated in the way we view the films. So, in that sense I'm incredibly proud to be part of this current moment in gay filmmaking.

M. Thank you, very much.

Works Cited

FILMS

Badlands. Dir. Terrence Malick. With Sissy Spacek and Martin Sheen. Warner/Pressman/Williams/Badlands, 1974.

Basic Instinct. Dir. Paul Verhoeven. With Michael Douglas and Sharon Stone. Guild/Carolco/Canal, 1992.

Beauty and the Beast. Dir. Jean Cocteau. With Jean Marais and Josette Day. Discina, 1946.

Beyond the Valley of the Dolls. Dir. Russ Meyer. With Edy Williams. TCF, 1970.

Blood and Roses. Dir. Roger Vadim. With Mel Ferrer, Annette Vadim and Elsa Martinelli. Documento,1971.

The Boys in the Band. Dir. William Friedkin. With Leonard Frey, Cliff Gorman, Reuben Greene, Robert La Tourneaux, and Laurence Luckinbill. CinemaCenter/ Leo, 1970.

Cat People. Dir. Jacques Tourneur. With Simone Simon, Kent Smith and Tim Conway. RKO, 1942.

Chimes at Midnight. Dir. Orson Welles. With Orson Welles, John Gielgud, Margaret Rutherford, Jeanne Moreau, and Fernando Rey. Internacional Films Española, 1966.

Cruising. Dir. William Friedkin. With Al Pacino, Paul Sorvino, Richard Cox, and Karen Allen. Lorimar, 1980.

The Detective. Dir. Gordon Douglas. With Frank Sinatra and Lee Remick. TCF/Arcola/Millfield, 1968.

Dracula. Dir. Tod Browning. With Bela Lugosi, Helen Chandler, Dwight Frye, Edward Van Sloan, and David Manners. Universal, 1931.

Bram Stoker's Dracula. Dir. Francis Ford Coppola. With Gary Oldman, Anthony Hopkins and Winona Ryder. Zoetrope Studios, 1992.

Dracula's Daughter. Dir. Lambert Hillyer. With Otto Kruger and Gloria Holden. Universal, 1936.

Fassbinder, Rainer Werner, dir. *Effi Briest*. With Hanna Schygulla and Wolfgang Schenk. Tango Film, 1974.

———. *Fox and His Friends*. With Rainer Werner Fassbinder and Peter Chatel. Tango Film, 1975.

———. *In a Year of Thirteen Moons*. With Volker Spengler and Ingrid Craven. Tango/Project/Filmverlag der Autoren, 1980.

———. *The Marriage of Maria Braun*. With Hanna Schygulla and Klaus Lowitsch. Albatross/Trio/WDR/FdA, 1979.

———. *Querelle*. With Brad Davis, Franco Nero, Dieter Schidor, and Günther Kaufmann. Planet/Albatross/ Gaumont, 1982.

The Fearless Vampire Killers. Dir. Roman Polanski. With Roman Polanski and Sharon Tate. MGM/Cadre Films/ Filmway, 1967.

Fireworks. Dir. Kenneth Anger. With Kenneth Anger. 1947.

The Fly. Dir. Kurt Neumann. With Vincent Price and Herbert Marshall. TCF, 1958.

The Fox. Dir. Mark Rydell. With Sandy Dennis, Anne Heywood and Keir Dullea. Warner/Raymond Stross/Motion Pictures International, 1968.

Genet, Jean, dir. *Un chant d'amour*. [No acting credits given.] Niko Kazatsakis, 1951.

Haynes, Todd, dir. *Poison*. With Edith Meeks, Scott Renderer, Jim Lyons and Larry Maxwell. Zeitgeist/Bronze Eye, 1991.

———. *Safe*. With Julianne Moore. Sony Classic, 1995.

———. *Superstar: The Karen Carpenter Story*. [No acting credits given. Produced privately by Todd Haynes in 1989; no commercial release.]

Hitchcock, Alfred, dir. *Psycho*. With Anthony Perkins, Vera Miles, John Gavin, and Janet Leigh. Shamley/Alfred Hitchcock, 1960.

———. *Rope*. With James Stewart, Cedric Hardwicke, Farley Granger and John Dall. Transatlantic, 1946.

———. *Strangers on a Train*. With Ruth Roman, Farley Granger and Robert Walker. Warner, 1951.

The Hunger. Dir. Tony Scott. With Catherine Deneuve and Susan Sarandon. MGM/UA, 1983.

I Married a Monster From Outer Space. Dir. Gene Fowler, Jr. With Tom Tryon and Gloria Talbot. Paramount, 1958.

Interview With The Vampire. Dir. Neil Jordan. With Tom Cruise, Brad Pitt, Christian Slater, Antonio Banderas and Kirsten Dunst. Geffen Pictures, 1994.

Invasion of the Body Snatchers. Dir. Don Siegel. With Kevin McCarthy and Dana Wynter. Allied Artists, 1956.

King Kong. Dir. John Guillermin. With Fay Wray and Bruce Cabot. RKO, 1933.

The Living End. Dir. Gregg araki. With Craig Glimore and Mike Dytri. Strand Releasing/Desperate Pictures, 1992.

Losey, Joseph, dir. *The Servant.* With Dirk Bogarde and James Fox. Springbok, 1963.

The Lost Language of Cranes. Dir. Nigel Finch. With Brian Cox, Eileen Atkins, Angus McFayden and Corey Parker.BBC/Lionheart/WNET, 1991.

Lust for a Vampire. Dir. Jimmy Sangster. With Michael Johnson, Suzanna Leigh, Yutte Stensgaard, and Ralph Bates. Hammer, 1970.

M. Dir. Fritz Lang. With Peter Lorre, Gustav Grundgens, Ellen Widman, and Inge Landgut. Nero Film, 1931.

The Maltese Falcon. Dir. John Huston. With Humphrey Bogart, Mary Astor, Sidney Greenstreet, Peter Lorre and Elisha Cook, Jr. Warner, 1941.

Maurice. Dir. James Ivory. With James Wilby, Rupert Graves, and Denholm Elliott. Cinecom/Merchant Ivory Productions, 1987.

The Mummy. Dir. Karl Freund. With Boris Karloff and David Manners. Universal, 1932.

Nadja. Dir. Michael Almereyda. With Elina Lowensohn, Peter Fonda, Galaxy Craze, Karl Geary, Suzy Amis, Martin Donovan II, and Jared Harris. Kino Link Company/October Films, 1994.

Naked Lunch. Dir. David Cronenberg. With Peter Weller, Judy Davis, Ian Holm, Julian Sands andRoy Scheider. Naked Lunch Productions/Recorded Pictures Company, 1992.

Night of the Living Dead. Dir. George Romero. With Judith O'Dea, Russell Streiner, and Duane Jones. Image Ten, 1968.

A Nightmare on Elm Street. Dir. Wes Craven. With John Saxon, Ronee Blakly, Robert Englund, and Johnny Depp. New Line/Media/Smart Egg/Elm Street Venture/ Robert Shaye, 1984.

Nosferatu. Dir. F. W. Murnau. With Max Schreck, Alexander Granach and Greta Schroeder. Prana, 1922.

One Million Years B.C. Dir. John Chaffey. With Raquel Welch. Hammer, 1966.

Paris is Burning. Dir. Jennie Livingston. With Pepper LaBeija and Dorian Corey. Off White Productions, 1990.

Parting Glances. Dir. Bill Sherwood. With Richard Ganoung, John Bolger and Steve Buscemi. Rondo, 1986.

Phantom of the Opera. Dir. Rupert Julian. With Lon Chaney, Sr., Mary Philbin, and Norman Kerry. Universal, 1925.

Pink Narcissus. Dir. Anonymous. With Bobby Kendall. 1971.

Postcards From America. Dir Steven McLean. With James Lyons, Olmo and
     Michael Tighe, Michael Ringer and Maggie Low. Produced by Craig Paull
     and Christine Vachon. 1994.

Preminger, Otto, dir. *Advise and Consent*. With Henry Fonda, Walter Pidgeon,
     Charles Laughton, and Don Murray. Columbia/Alpha-Alpina/Otto
     Preminger, 1962.

————. *Laura*. With Gene Tierney, Dana Andrews and Clifton Webb. TCF,
     1944.

The Searchers. Dir. John Ford. With John Wayne, Jeffrey Hunter and Natalie
     Wood. Warner/C.V. Whitney, 1956.

Serving in Silence: The Margarethe Cammermeyer Story. With Glenn Close and
     Judy Davis. NBC, 6 February, 1995. TriStar Television, 1995.

Silence of the Lambs. Dir. Jonathan Demme. With Anthony Hopkins and Jodie
     Foster. Rank/Orion, 1990.

Staircase. Dir. Stanley Donen. With Rex Harrison and Richard Burton.
     TCF/Stanley Donen, 1969.

Suddenly Last Summer. Dir. Joseph Mankiewizc. With Elizabeth Taylor,
     Montgomery Clift and Katherine Hepburn. Columbia/Horizon, 1959.

The Sugarland Express. Dir. Steven Spielberg. With Goldie Hawn and William
     Atherton. Universal, 1974.

Swoon. Dir. Tom Kalin. With Daniel Schlachet and Craig Chester. Produced by
     Tom Kalin, James Schamus, Christine Vachon, Peter Wentworth, and
     Lauren Zalaznick. 1992.

Tales of the City. Dir. Alistair Reid. With Olympia Dukakis, Donald Moffat,
     Laura Linney, and Chloe Webb. Propaganda/Working Title/Channel
     4/American Playhouse/KQED, 1993.

The Terminator. Dir. James Cameron. With Arnold Schwarzenegger and Linda
     Hamilton. Orion/Hemdale/Pacific Western, 1984.

Terminator Two: Judgement Day. Dir. James Cameron. With Arnold
     Schwarzenegger. Carolco Pictures/Pacific Western, 1991.

Thelma and Louise. Dir. Ridley Scott. With Susan Sarandonand Geena Davis.
     MGM/UA, 1992.

The Thing. Dir. Howard Hawks. With Kenneth Tobey, Margaret Sheridan, and
     James Arness. Universal/Laurance Turman/David Foster, 1951.

The Times of Harvey Milk. Dir. Robert Epstein. Cinecom, 1984.

Treut, Monika, dir. *Female Misbehavior*. With Camille Paglia and Annie
     Sprinkle. Hyena Films,1992.

————. (Co-director with Elfi Mikesch). *Seduction: The Cruel Woman*. With
     Mechthild Grossman and Udo Kier. Hyena Films, 1985.

————. *Virgin Machine*. With Annie Sprinkle. Hyena Films, 1988.

Twins of Evil. Dir. John Hough. With Madeline Collinson and Peter Cushing.
     Rank/Hammer, 1971.

The Vampire Lovers. Dir. Roy Baker. With Ingrid Pitt and Peter Cushing.
     Hammer, 1970.

Van Sant, Gus, dir. *My Own Private Idaho*. With Keanu Reeves, William Richert, Udo Kier and River Phoenix. New Line, 1991.

Victim. Dir. Basil Dearden. With Dirk Bogarde, Sylvia Syms, and Dennis Price. Parkway, 1959.

Von Praunheim, Rosa, dir. *Army of Lovers: Or, Revolt of the Perverts.* With Rosa Von Praunheim. First Run Features, 1972.

———. *I Am My Own Woman*. With Charlotte Von Mahlsdorf, Jens Taschner and Ichgola Androgyn. Cinevista, 1992.

———. *It is Not the Homosexual Who is Perverse, But the Society in Which He Lives.* First Run Features, 1970.

A Walk on the Wild Side. Dir. Edward Dmytryk. With Barbara Stanwyck and Laurence Harvey. Columbia/Famous Artists, 1962.

The War of the Worlds. Dir. Byron Haskin. With Gene Barry, Ann Robinson, and Les Tremayne. Paramount/ George Pal, 1953.

Whale, James, dir. *The Bride of Frankenstein*. With Colin Clive, Elsa Lancaster, Ernest Thesiger, Valerie Hobson, Dwight Frye, and Una O'Connor. Universal, 1935.

———. *Frankenstein*. With Boris Karloff, Colin Clive, Edward Van Sloan, and Dwight Frye. Universal, 1931.

———. *The Invisible Man*. With Claude Rains, Henry Travers, Gloria Stuart, and Una O'Connor. Universal, 1933.

White Zombie. Dir. Victor Halperin. With Bela Lugosi and Madge Bellamy. American Securities Corp., 1932.

Winter Kills. Dir. William Richert. With Jeff Bridges, John Huston and Anthony Perkins. Avco Embassy/Winter Gold, 1979.

The Wolf Man. Dir. George Waggner. With Lon Chaney, Jr., Claude Rains and Evelyn Ankers. Universal, 1941.

REVIEWS

Anderson, John. "The Final Cut." *New York Newsday*. 4 April, 1991: 73.

Ansen, David. Review of *The Living End*. *Newsweek*. August 31, 1992, v120, n9: 68.

Assayas, Olivier. "L'Enfer de Brest." Review of *Querelle*. *Cahiers du cinéma*. N340, Oct. 1983, Pp. 27-30.

Berger, Maurice. Review of *Poison*. *Artforum*. Oct. 1991, v30, n2: 17.

Canby, Vincent. Review of *It is Not the Homosexual Who is Perverse, But the Society in Which He Lives*. *The New York Times*. National Edition. V127, Nov. 25, 1977: C-10+.

Corliss, Richard. Review of *Poison*. *Time*. May 13, 1991, v137, n19: 69.

Dargis, Manohla. Review of *Female Misbehavior*. *Village Voice*. V38, April 27, 1993: 62+.

Franke, Lizzie. Review of *The Living End*. *Sight and Sound*. Feb.1993, v3, n2: 49+.

Fuller, Graham. "Gus Van Sant: Swimming Against the Current." In Gus Van Sant, *Even Cowgirls Get the Blues* and *My Own Private Idaho*. Boston: Faber and Faber, 1993.

Giles, Jane. Review of *Un Chant D'amour*. *Artforum*. January, 1988: 102.

Greenberg, Harvey R. Review of *My Own Private Idaho*. *Film Quarterly*. Fall 1992, v46, n1: 24+.

Greenberg, Steve. "No More Tales." *The Advocate*. May 31, 1994, Pp. 59-61.

Handelman, David. "Gus Van Sant's Northwest Passage." Review of *My Own Private Idaho*. *Rolling Stone*, Oct. 31, 1991, n616: 61.

Hansen, David. Review of *I Am My Own Woman*. *Variety*. V349, December 7, 1992, 72.

―――. "Prince Hal in Portland: the risk-taking director of *Drugstore Cowboy* makes a bold new movie on his hometown streets." Review of *My Own Private Idaho*. *Newsweek*. April 15, 1991, v117, n15: 68.

Hoberman, J. Review of *Army of Lovers: or, Revolt of the Perverts*. *Village Voice*. V24, December 10, 1979, Pp. 60-61.

―――. Review of *It is Not the Homosexual Who is Perverse, But the Situation in Which He Lives*. *Village Voice*. V22, Nov. 28, 1977, Pp50-54.

Holden, Stephen. Review of *I Am My Own Woman*. *The New York Times*. National Edition. April 29, 1994, v143: C-15.

Isherwood, Charles. "The Men Behind Glenn." *The Advocate*. Issue 672/673, January 24, 1995, Pp. 70-73.

James, Caryn. "Politics nurtures *Poison*. (Todd Haynes' film spurs controversy." Review of *Poison*. *The New York Times*. National Edition. April 14, 1991, v140, Sec. 2: H-15+.

Jenkins, Nicholas. Review of *Poison*. *Times Literary Supplement*. November 15, 1991, n4624: 19+.

Johnson, Brian D. Review of *My Own Private Idaho*. *Maclean's*. Oct. 28, 1991, v104, n43: 101.

Maslin Janet. Review of *The Living End*. *New York Times*. April 3, 1992, v141: C-1.

Monk, Claire. Review of *Verführung: die grausame Frau*. *Sight and Sound*. NS3, Issue 5. May 1993. Pp. 59-60.

Nickles, Elizabeth. "Overripe Beauty." Review of *Querelle*. *Saturday Review*. May/June, 1983, Pp. 20-21.

Pitman, Randy. Review of *Poison*. *Library Journal*. July 1992, v117, n12: 144.

Travers, Peter. Review of *The Living End*. *Rolling Stone*. September 3, 1992, n368: 75.

BOOKS AND JOURNALS

"AIDS and Bathhouses." Narr. Joe Neel. Dir. Marieka Partridge. Exec. Prod. Ellen Weiss. All Things Considered. NPR, Washington, D.C., 1 June, 1995.

Altman, Dennis. *Homosexual Oppression and Liberation.* New York: New York University Press, 1993.

Aristotle. *Poetics.* In *The Complete Works of Aristotle.* The Revised Oxford Translation. Vol. 2. Jonathan Barnes, ed. Princeton, N.J.: Princeton University Press, 1990.

Bettelheim, Bruno. *The Uses of Enchantment: The Meaning and Importance of Fairy Tales.* New York: Vintage Books, 1977.

Browning, Frank. *The Culture of Desire: Paradox and Perversity in Gay Lives Today.* New York: Crown Publishers, Inc., 1993.

Cook, David A. *A History of Narrative Film.* Second Edition. New York: W. W. Norton & Company, 1990.

Corrigan, Timothy. *A Cinema Without Walls: Movies and Culture After Vietnam.* New Brunswick, N.J.: Rutgers University Press, 1991.

Dollimore, Jonathan. *Sexual Dissidence: Augustine to Wilde, Freud to Foucault.* Oxford: Clarendon Press, 1992.

Dubin, Steven C. *Arresting Images: Impolitic Art and Uncivil Actions.* London: Routledge, 1992.

Dyer, Richard. *The Matter of Images: Essays on Representation.* New York: Routledge, 1993.

———. *Now You See It: Studies on Lesbian and Gay Film.* London and New York: Routledge, 1990.

Evans, Arthur. *Jean Cocteau and His Films of Orphic Identity.* Philadelphia: Arts Alliance Press, 1977.

Frye, Northrop. *Anatomy of Criticism.* Princeton: Princeton University Press, 1973.

Genet, Jean. *Miracle of the Rose.* Trans. Bernard Frechtman. New York: Grove Weidenfeld, 1966.

———. *Our Lady of the Flowers.* Trans. Bernard Frechtman. New York: Grove Weidenfeld, 1963.

———. *Querelle.* Trans. Anselm Hollo. New York: Grove Weidenfeld, 1974.

———. *The Thief's Journal.* Trans. Bernard Frechtman. New York: Grove Press, Inc., 1964.

Giles, Jane. *The cinema of Jean Genet: Un Chant d'amour.* London: British Film Institute, 1991.

Grundmann, Roy. "The Fantasies We Live By: Bad Boys in *Swoon* and *The Living End.*" *Cineaste,* Fall, 1992, XIX: iv.

Huet, Marie Hélène. *Monstrous Imagination.* Cambridge: Harvard University Press, 1993.

Knight, Julia. "Off Our Backs." *Sight and Sound.* v2 n2, June, 1992, pp. 30-35.

Kort, Michele. "Marathon Woman: An Interview With Patricia Nell Warren." *The Advocate.* May 31, 1994, Issue 656: 50+.

Malkan, Jeffrey. "Aggressive Text: Murder and the Fine Arts Revisited." *Mosaic* (Winnipeg). Winter, 1990, v23, n1, Pp. 101-107.

Mulvey, Laura. "Film and Visual Pleasure." In *Film Theory and Criticism: Introductory Readings*. Gerald Mast and Marshall Cohen, eds. New York: Oxford University Press, 1985.

Oswald, Laura. *Jean Genet and the Semiotics of Performance*. Bloomington: Indiana University Press, 1989.

Raab, Kurt, and Peters, Karsten. *Die Sehnsucht des Rainer Werner Fassbinders*. München: C. Bertelsmann Verlag, GmbH, 1982.

Rechy, John. *The Sexual Outlaw*. New York: Grove Weidenfeld, 1987.

Rickels, Laurence. "It's a wound-erful life." *Artforum*.V32, December, 1993, Pp. 47-49.

Russo, Vito. *The Celluloid Closet: Homosexuality in the Movies*. Revised Edition. New York: Harper and Row, 1987.

Shaviro, Steven. *The Cinematic Body*. Vol.2 of *Theory Out of Bounds*. Minneapolis: University of Minnesota Press, 1993.

Steegmuller, Francis. *Cocteau: A Biography*. Boston: Little, Brown and Company, 1970.

Stoker, Bram. *Dracula*. New York: Signet/Penguin Books, 1992.

Teal, Don. *The Gay Militants*. New York: St. Martin's Press, 1971.

Tyler, Parker. *Screening the Sexes: Homosexuality in the Movies*. Garden City: Anchor Books, 1973.

White, Edmund. *Genet: A Biography*. New York: Alfred A. Knopf, 1993.

Wyatt, Justin. "Cinematic/Sexual Transgression: An Interview With Todd Haynes." *Film Quarterly*. V46, n3, Spring 1993: 6+.

Index

About the Author

MICHAEL WILLIAM SAUNDERS is Assistant Part-Time Professor of English and German at Kennesaw State University, Kennesaw, Georgia. He teaches courses in rhetoric, literature, composition, drama and film. To make ends meet he also works full-time as a software instructor while developing writing projects after hours. He is currently working on a translation of Christoph Martin Wieland's *Die Geschichte des Agathon* and a series of short stories.

ISBN 0-275-95761-6

90000>

9 780275 957612

HARDCOVER BAR CODE